A CONCISE
BUSINESS GUIDE TO
CLIMATE CHANGE

A CONCISE
BUSINESS GUIDE TO
CLIMATE
CHANGE

What Managers, Executives, and Students Need to Know

GUNNAR TRUMBULL

HARVARD BUSINESS REVIEW PRESS

BOSTON, MASSACHUSETTS

HBR Press Quantity Sales Discounts

Harvard Business Review Press titles are available at significant quantity discounts when purchased in bulk for client gifts, sales promotions, and premiums. Special editions, including books with corporate logos, customized covers, and letters from the company or CEO printed in the front matter, as well as excerpts of existing books, can also be created in large quantities for special needs.

For details and discount information for both print and ebook formats, contact booksales@harvardbusiness.org, tel. 800-988-0886, or www.hbr.org/bulksales.

Copyright 2025 Gunnar Trumbull

All rights reserved

Printed in the United States of America

10 9 8 7 6 5 4 3 2 1

No part of this publication may be reproduced, stored in or introduced into a retrieval system, or transmitted, in any form, or by any means (electronic, mechanical, photocopying, recording, or otherwise), without the prior permission of the publisher. Requests for permission should be directed to permissions@harvardbusiness.org, or mailed to Permissions, Harvard Business School Publishing, 60 Harvard Way, Boston, Massachusetts 02163.

The web addresses referenced in this book were live and correct at the time of the book's publication but may be subject to change.

Cataloging-in-Publication data is forthcoming.

ISBN: 978-1-64782-542-3
eISBN: 978-1-64782-543-0

The paper used in this publication meets the requirements of the American National Standard for Permanence of Paper for Publications and Documents in Libraries and Archives Z39.48-1992.

For Julio Rotemberg,
colleague and friend

CONTENTS

CHAPTER 1

INTRODUCTION   1

How to Use This Book   2
A Role for Leadership   4
Concluding Thoughts   6

CHAPTER 2

FIRMS CONFRONT CLIMATE CHANGE   9

Strategy   10
Organization   18
Leadership   22
Accounting   24
Regulation   29
Concluding Thoughts   32

CHAPTER 3

CLIMATE SCIENCE   35

Climate Modeling   37
The Energy Balance Model   38
The General Circulation Model   42
Integrated Assessment Models   52
From Climate to Weather   55
Rising Tides, Stronger Storms   59
Concluding Thoughts   61

CONTENTS

CHAPTER 4

THE MARKET FOR CARBON 63

Sources of Carbon Emissions 64

The Social Cost of Carbon 67

The Discounting Debate 69

A Carbon Budget 73

Carbon Offsets 76

Offsets and Their Critics 78

Concluding Thoughts 81

CHAPTER 5

GREEN ENERGY TRANSITION 83

Power, Energy, and CO_2 84

Petroleum 85

Natural Gas and Coal 88

Fossil Fuels and Climate Change 90

Renewable Sources 92

Peak and Base Load 94

The Cost and Benefits of Renewables 96

Concluding Thoughts 99

CHAPTER 6

POLICY RESPONSE TO CLIMATE CHANGE 103

The UN Framework 105

Regional Approaches to Climate Change 113

Concluding Thoughts 122

CHAPTER 7

FINAL THOUGHTS 125

Glossary 129

Notes 147

Index 149

Acknowledgments 161

About the Author 163

A CONCISE
BUSINESS GUIDE TO
CLIMATE
CHANGE

CHAPTER 1

INTRODUCTION

Business leaders around the world are being called on to respond to the challenges of a changing climate. By 2023, half of the world's two thousand largest companies had adopted operational plans to reduce their carbon emissions. Pressure for change comes from a wide range of sources: activist investors, concerned customers, employees, and also increasingly from companies' own CEOs and boards of directors. How a leadership team responds will have profound strategic, operational, and reputational consequences that can also be hard to predict.

Yet this is not an area in which most corporate leaders feel comfortable or have experience. Given this limitation, many companies will rely on outside experts to help them navigate the climate transition. Virtually all global consulting and accounting firms have retooled to provide advice in this area. They foresee climate consulting, alongside artificial intelligence, as *the* dominant growth areas for their businesses in the coming decade. However, even with help from outside experts, business leaders

2   A CONCISE BUSINESS GUIDE TO CLIMATE CHANGE

require a base level of knowledge of climate change to navigate this challenge.

That is because an effective response will require leadership from the top. It may seem expedient for a CEO to task an operational manager or outside consultant with designing and meeting a company's new carbon emissions targets. But that reflex is usually a mistake. The changes necessary to reduce or eliminate carbon emissions have an impact on every part of a company; they must be crafted with the broader strategy of the firm in mind. Only the top leadership of a firm can coordinate this kind of response effectively.

The physics of climate change and our policy responses to it constitute a fairly complex set of technical issues and tools. Newcomers to these topics are likely to feel uncertain due to their lack of familiarity, and this uncertainty can give them a sense of insecurity and vulnerability as they craft their responses. Furthermore, while the science of climate change is well established, it is an area of expertise that is rife with misdirection and outright misinformation. What claims about climate change are grounded in science, and which are not? Which sources can be trusted? A foundation of knowledge can save business leaders from misleading or wrong advice.

How to Use This Book

This guide introduces basic climate science, the economics of carbon markets, government policy responses, conventional and green energy, and business approaches to decarbonization. It is intended to be a trusted companion as business leaders confront the challenges of responding and adapting to climate change.

We begin in chapter 2 with the most pressing question for most business leaders: How should firms approach the challenge of reducing their greenhouse gas emissions? An exhaustive answer to this

INTRODUCTION   3

question lies outside the scope of this short book. Instead, we introduce a framework to guide business leaders as they begin to make decisions related to decarbonization. The framework explores the different operational dimensions of a firm's climate response, captured in the SOLAR framework. SOLAR provides a guide to the five primary dimensions along which to evaluate the risks and opportunities of decarbonization: **s**trategy, **o**rganization, **l**eadership, **a**ccounting, and **r**egulation. As these categories suggest, an effective corporate climate response affects many of the core functions of a firm.

Chapter 3 introduces the basic science of climate change. Why are global temperatures rising? Why are some areas experiencing heightened rainfall, while others are suffering ever greater aridity? This chapter introduces the geophysical models we use to understand the rising global temperature. It explains how global air and water flows cause regional weather conditions. The mechanisms laid out in this chapter represent the current scientific consensus. They are presented in a clear, accurate, but accessible way.

Chapter 4 addresses the economics of greenhouse gas emissions. Where do the emissions come from? What is the most efficient way for governments to reduce emissions? In particular, it explores the role of markets in reducing carbon emissions, with a focus on carbon taxes and cap-and-trade schemes.

Chapter 5 looks at the green energy transition. Energy markets today have reached an inflection point at which renewable sources have become price-competitive with traditional fossil fuels. Yet important questions remain. How is the global energy system likely to change as we transition to renewable sources of power? How fast will the transition occur, and what will it mean for the political economy of rich and developing countries? This chapter presents what we know about the energy transition that is occurring right now.

Chapter 6 focuses on government responses to climate change. It explains the origins of global coordination through the Intergovernmental

Panel on Climate Change, and the role of the Kyoto Protocol and Paris Agreement in supporting national responses. It then focuses on the policy response in three critical regions: the European Union, the United States, and China.

A Role for Leadership

Climate change is a big problem. It will require ingenuity and large allocations of capital to address. That means the climate transition also poses significant risk. Incumbent firms are torn between two options. On the one hand, they can make early investments in technologies and products that will point the way forward in decarbonizing their sector. This puts them out front, where both risks and rewards associated with new products and markets may be high. On the other hand, firms may wait for competitors in their sector to test the decarbonization waters. But this path creates risks as well, as competitors build a lead in technologies that may fundamentally transform sectoral competition. A strategy of climate catch-up poses its own challenges, and firms that delay risk losing their competitive edge.

Navigating the green transition will require that we shepherd scarce resources. Regions with the most abundant renewable sources will become targets for new investments. Manufacturers are already flocking to secure power purchase agreements from low-carbon hydro sources in northern Scandinavia and northeast Brazil. Where solar and wind are especially strong and reliable—West Texas, Morocco, Chile, the Gobi Desert—new green industrial hubs are quickly emerging. Batteries to power new electric vehicle fleets will put strains on natural resources but also create enormous opportunities for minerals mining and processing. Similarly, clean energy companies are scouring the world for workers who have the skills they will require to support the transition, creating opportunities for those with relevant skills.

Yet the most valuable and potentially scarcest resource through this transition is likely to be effective and thoughtful leadership. Sector by sector, we face the kind of transformation that will challenge the mettle and vision of our global managerial class. This book is intended to support these leaders as they begin their decarbonization journey.

Given the broad-based nature of the transition we are facing, the range of roles in which these leaders operate is unusually broad. Within firms, climate leadership is no longer solely the responsibility of sustainability officers. Functional areas ranging from finance, accounting, and marketing to product development are all now on the front line of corporate decarbonization efforts. In many cases, corporate boards of directors are making critical decisions around decarbonization that may be far from their traditional areas of competency. Investors are also increasingly being challenged to balance the social purpose of climate response against the returns to institutional pools of capital such as pension funds—and to justify publicly the decisions they are making. Even major nongovernmental organizations such as the World Wildlife Fund are increasingly interacting directly with firms to monitor and support their decarbonization efforts.

Our approach to climate change is also now global in scope. In the new multipolar world of climate response, green innovations and technologies can be found virtually everywhere. Chinese firms lead the world in some of the key renewable energy technologies, including batteries, photovoltaic panels, and electric vehicles. US entrepreneurs are at the cutting edge of new technologies to support geothermal and fusion generation. Europe has been a leader in decarbonization, setting some of the most aggressive emissions standards in the world, along with a carbon border tax that will mean that many suppliers that sell in Europe will increasingly have to meet Europe's standards. India is pursuing a green industrial policy that it hopes will ensure energy independence and make it a leader in low-carbon global supply chains. Leaders from all of these geographies—and more—are being called on to tackle the challenges of climate change.

I am convinced that firms that act decisively and thoughtfully to decarbonize will reap vast rewards. For many sectors, they are staring down a generational opportunity to restructure competition. Sectoral leadership is up for grabs. New generations of industrial wealth will be created. One powerful reason for firms to move quickly to tackle decarbonization is to ensure that they are in the game. By building leadership skills early, they can be thoughtful about the risks and opportunities that present themselves through this transition. I hope that this book can provide a starting point for this journey.

Concluding Thoughts

In my research and teaching on climate change, I interact with a lot of students and business leaders who are despairing of our ability to respond adequately to the challenge. They worry about weak or ineffective government policies, and the entrenched economic interests that perpetuate them. I don't, however, share this pessimism.

The source of my optimism comes from the business leaders who are at the forefront of solving the problem. Our response to climate change will depend critically on firms' operational changes. Governments can design incentives that make it more attractive for companies to reduce carbon emissions, but ultimately it is companies and their leadership that will take the key decisions that will solve this problem. And the business leaders who are driving this change have an infectious optimism. While they acknowledge that the challenges we face are daunting, they also clearly relish the opportunities that come with tackling challenging goals.

One source of their excitement, I think, is that they see potentially huge benefits in a society based on renewable energy. For all of their advantages, oil and coal are far too expensive to support economic development in poor countries. In fact, governments in most poor countries provide generous gasoline subsidies in order to bring this critical input within financial reach of average citizens. Yet, within a generation, abundant and cheap renewable energy could transform those economies. Technological advances in solar, wind, and battery storage have the potential to drive economic dynamism in regions that were left behind during the first, fossil-fuel-driven industrialization. These new energy sources also tend to be nonpolluting and relatively robust to environmental and political disruption. Widespread adoption of renewable energy sources could even begin to rebalance geopolitical dependencies that have long been rooted in the vagaries of where fossil fuels have been abundant.

Such possibilities raise the prospect that a new green economy might provide a pathway to rectify historical injustices perpetrated during the age of coal- and oil-driven industrialization. This historical context emphasizes the importance of social justice in our response to climate change. Traditionally marginalized groups—indigenous peoples of the Arctic, or poor fishing communities of coastal Bangladesh—are also frequently those that are most vulnerable to changing climate conditions. As our economies transition away from fossil fuels, other groups will become vulnerable. Coal miners who were already economically marginalized, for example, now face a threat to their very livelihoods. These realities imply that our response to climate change is inexorably linked to dimensions of societal justice. As one South African executive explained to me about the green transition in his country, "Without a *just* transition, there will be *no* climate transition."

The project to decarbonize our economies bears with it both the challenge and the opportunity of addressing profound existing societal ills.

The potential for broad societal benefits from decarbonization is mirrored by the potential benefits to individual companies. Firms that have set out on a journey to eliminate their carbon emissions have commonly found that the necessary reforms also help to make their businesses more efficient. Nestlé, for example, estimates that it can reduce its greenhouse gas emissions by half at zero net cost, since many of the operational reforms will ultimately pay for themselves. Climate entrepreneurs are even more optimistic. They see endless opportunity that will arise through the energy transition. As one leader in a green energy startup explained to me, "If we do things that are hard enough, the profits will follow."

While these optimistic scenarios will not play out for every company, what is clear is that adding climate as a management goal has helped leaders to think more broadly and creatively about their processes and products. And it is telling that the leaders who are closest to the problem—those who are on the front lines of response—are also the ones who are most optimistic about solving the problem. Humans tend to turn away from problems that seem too big, too daunting. We need to resist this impulse. My hope is that a better understanding of climate change, of its human and physical causes, will empower our leaders to confront the challenge and find beneficial and profitable paths forward.

CHAPTER 2

FIRMS CONFRONT CLIMATE CHANGE

The primary audience for this book is executives facing the challenge of crafting a corporate response to climate change. In later chapters, we address the scientific and economic content they should be familiar with. We start, however, by providing guidance and exploring questions and challenges that corporations face as they are designing their response. This chapter lays out a conceptual framework to help structure that response. The goal of this framework is not to tell firms what to do, but to guide their discussions as they develop a strategy that works for them.

The framework identifies five areas in which responding to climate change interacts with the core functions of the firm. These areas are strategy, organization, leadership, accounting, and regulation. As a memory device, they spell out SOLAR. As these categories make clear, virtually no function of a firm will be untouched by considerations related to climate change. Executed properly, a firm's climate response can allow its leadership to reposition and restructure the firm for success in a new phase of competition oriented toward a low-carbon economy. It will help corporate leaders to identify potentially profitable paths forward, while also assessing what climate change is likely to mean for the structure and profitability of their sector. I lay out the SOLAR framework in more detail in the following sections.

Strategy

Any meaningful climate effort must begin with a company's strategy. In fact, I would argue that companies that are not thinking about climate change from a strategic perspective are not really dealing with it in a serious or useful way. As managers look forward, there are few sectors where climate adaptation and decarbonization do not have the potential to change or even fundamentally reshape the competitive landscape. How companies respond to that coming strategic challenge will depend on a range of factors, including the sector, organizational capabilities, regulatory framework, and others. Critically, no single solution will fit all firms or sectors. Yet, even as firms plot different strategic responses to climate change, the ways in which they evaluate and define those responses must take into account a common set of considerations.

These common strategic considerations are summarized in a second mnemonic device, the ACCESS template. The corresponding categories of strategic analysis are: **a**ssessment, **c**ustomers, **c**ompetition, **e**mployees, **s**uppliers, and **s**cenarios. The ACCESS template provides a checklist for evaluating firm-level strategic responses to climate change. We review each of these categories next.

Assessment of the Physical Risk of Climate Change

The first time many companies confront climate as a business reality is when they realize the impact climate change will have, and perhaps is already having, on their business operations. They may rely on climate-vulnerable inputs. They may have infrastructure that is at risk from climate-driven extreme weather. Or they may face higher insurance costs due to greater flooding or fire risks. As firms recognize these new environmental challenges, and make investments to adapt to them, they also confront the reality that they are themselves contributing to climate change. Starbucks, for example, the largest coffee chain in the world, faces a dramatic climate-related threat to its major input: coffee beans. Our climate projections suggest that the amount of land that remains viable for coffee crops will decline significantly by 2050. That agricultural reality, and the potentially existential threat it posed for its core product, led the Starbucks leaders to think more carefully about their own impact on the climate, and to lay out plans for a carbon-neutral green coffee future.

This experience is not uncommon. In general, organizations facing greater operational risk from climate change have also tended to engage more aggressively in reducing their own climate footprint. In many cases, the direct physical risk serves as a wake-up call to reassess their broader climate strategy. For example, the US Navy realized in the early 2000s that its global network of naval bases was especially vulnerable to climate-driven sea-level rise and storm surge. The US Navy was also one of the largest institutional users of fossil fuels in the world, meaning it was contributing to the very climate problem that threatened it. Ray Mabus, secretary of the navy at the time, decided that the US Navy should play a part in reducing its climate risk. In 2009, he announced that the US Navy would shift to 50 percent alternative fuel sources by 2020, with an emphasis on biofuels. The move helped to create a market for sustainable bio-based fuels, driving investment and innovation among fuel suppliers, while also making the US Navy less dependent on global oil prices, and less vulnerable to holdup from petroleum-rich states.

Customers

One of the most pressing drivers of decarbonization can come from customers: either end consumers concerned about their consumption impact on the climate, or corporate customers that wish to decarbonize their supply chains. The range of companies this may affect is broad. Any firm selling in Europe, for example, is facing pressure to plan for decarbonization.

Companies that sell directly to consumers must pay attention to their attitudes toward climate change, noting any potential willingness to pay a premium for climate-friendly products. Research into customers' willingness to pay has generated a range of estimates, although it appears to be growing over time. For example, the accounting firm PricewaterhouseCoopers found in a 2024 consumer survey that 80 percent of customers were willing to pay more for climate-friendly products.[1] But that green premium may not be very large. A contemporaneous survey by the consulting firm BCG found that only 10 percent of Americans were willing to pay a 10 percent green premium, for example, while half were willing to pay a 3 percent green premium.[2] Yet even customers who are unwilling to pay a green premium are increasingly selecting products and brands that offer a climate benefit. In some cases, consumers may select green products over similarly priced alternatives, even though they are not willing to pay more. In other cases, consumers may choose energy-efficient products in the expectation that they will have lower lifetime operating costs. This may be relevant for purchases of automobiles or refrigerators, for example. These factors mean that direct-to-consumer producers must think carefully about the present and future demand they will face for climate-friendly products.

Many firms are suppliers for other firms, and for them the calculus for decarbonization may be different. In some cases, they face broader regulatory challenges and opportunities. Providers of energy-intensive inputs like steel and chemicals, for example, either must comply with Europe's Emissions Trading System if they operate in Europe or face Europe's Carbon Border Adjustment Mechanism (CBAM) if they do not but plan to sell in Europe. The scope of the CBAM and the number of covered sectors is likely to expand to new product categories over time. Beyond formal carbon taxation schemes, there are other reasons to offer lower-carbon options to their customers. Many companies globally have announced net-zero emissions targets, and they are increasingly looking to their suppliers to reduce emissions on inputs into their own products and services. When companies claim the emissions reductions of their suppliers toward their own carbon abatement targets, they refer to those reductions as carbon insets. Many consumer-facing firms are relying heavily on carbon insets generated by their suppliers to meet their 2030 greenhouse gas (GHG) emissions reductions targets.

Even companies that do not currently have emissions goals for their suppliers may change their priorities and decide they will request them in the future. Walmart, for example, has committed to specific emissions reduction targets from its own operations, but not for those of its suppliers. Nonetheless, it has worked with its suppliers to reduce their emissions, and those that are able to provide greater emissions reductions from their own operations are likely to secure a strong position as Walmart suppliers. Over the longer term, successful suppliers must be prepared to accompany their customers on their decarbonization journey as it evolves.

Competition

Climate change is disrupting the conventional logic of competition in many markets. In some sectors, where all competitors are being asked to move toward green practices, greater climate transparency coupled with GHG emission reduction targets can afford a source of differentiation relative to competitors. The Belgian chemicals producer Solvay, for example, has begun developing low-weight composite components for aviation and autos. As its customers have increasingly emphasized energy efficiency for their products, Solvay's new components are enjoying a strong market advantage.

In other cases, former commodity markets are being segmented between traditional and green supplies. We observe this logic in the palm oil industry. Normally sold as a commodity with relatively low margins, Indonesian palm oil has come under attack in Europe for the climate impact of its sourcing practices. The biggest concerns are forest clearing and the destruction of peat bogs, both of which constitute some of the largest stocks of terrestrial carbon in the world. Faced with a threat from the European Union to ban all palm oil that cannot guarantee a low-carbon footprint, Indonesia's largest producer—Golden Agri-Resources—is implementing full climate traceability to allay the concerns of its European customers. At the same time, other Indonesian producers that sell primarily into Asian markets are, for now, *not* placing as much emphasis on climate impact.

In some markets, producers can expect to be paid a green premium for low-carbon technologies and products—but that situation is relatively rare. More commonly, customer demands for carbon accounting and GHG emission reduction are unlikely to be matched with greater willingness to pay. Even products that earn a green premium in the near term are likely to lose that revenue advantage as customers demand higher standards of decarbonization from all producers. Ultimately, dimensions of climate response are set to become an element of the competitive landscape, although at different times in different sectors. Suppliers and producers that cannot provide this capability will be passed over for competitors that can.

Employees

Firms that focus on climate awareness and embrace a decarbonization trajectory are increasingly enjoying advantages in attracting and retaining skilled workers. This is especially true of the younger and more highly educated workforce, where concern about climate change tends to be higher than among older workers. A 2021 survey of British college students found that 20 percent would turn down a job offer at a company that was recognized to be contributing to climate change.[3] And among European workers eighteen to twenty-four years old, half said they would be willing to leave their company based on inaction on climate.[4] Polls also find that more highly educated workers are more concerned about climate than are lower-skilled workers.[5] For firms that rely on a highly skilled labor force, especially in sectors where those skills are scarce, setting a corporate climate target and accompanying policies can help to attract and retain the right workers. In the race to secure skills that will be needed to decarbonize manufacturing, for example, companies that start first will enjoy greater ability to attract and retain the necessary skills.

Suppliers

Any firm that sets out on a decarbonization journey must decide whether to focus on the carbon impact of the firm itself (Scope 1 and 2), or to include the carbon content of the product it sells (Scope 3). (For more on carbon accounting, see the section on accounting later in this chapter.) The latter option implies that it will minimize not just its own carbon footprint, but also those of firms along the supply chain from which it purchases inputs. For many producers, the supply chain may constitute the bulk of emissions embedded in the products they sell. Decarbonizing the supply chain may be relatively more or less challenging depending on the capabilities and structure of a company's supply chain. Two considerations are critical for assessing whether and how to approach supply chain emissions.

First, how much control do you have over your supply chain? Larger buyers may have significant leverage over their suppliers, and their suppliers in turn are typically willing to make important investments in the understanding that their anchor client will value them. Dominant buyers may also be able to reduce the risk of supply chain decarbonization by locking in long-term sales contracts, called offtake agreements, from their main suppliers. BMW, for example, signed a multiyear offtake agreement with the green steel startup Stegra in order to support the costly investments that Stegra was making to decarbonize this critical auto input. Similar offtake agreements are supporting battery manufacturers and sustainable aviation fuel suppliers. For smaller buyers, the behavior of larger competitors will likely determine the trajectory of supply chain decarbonization. If large competitors are pushing their suppliers to decarbonize, smaller buyers may be able to piggyback off of and reinforce their efforts.

Second, can your suppliers pursue low-cost abatement or sequestration? For companies setting a net-zero target, extending their target to Scope 3 emissions that include their suppliers may offer an easier path to quick emissions reductions if their suppliers offer possibilities for low-cost carbon emissions reduction and/or sequestration. Nestlé, for example, is the largest dairy customer in the world. It buys, directly or through intermediaries, from over 600,000 dairy farmers globally. And GHG emissions from dairy farming account for 80 percent of the carbon footprint of Nestlé's products. By announcing a Scope 3 emissions target, Nestlé has been able to work with its network of dairy farmers to change their farming practices in ways that reduce farming emissions at relatively low cost. Nestlé then claims the resulting carbon soil sequestration and enteric methane emissions reduction as part of its own emissions reduction plan.[6]

As the Nestlé case suggests, corporate and regulatory efforts to reduce emissions in a single market, as in Europe, can potentially have global impacts. This in turn creates opportunities and risks for developing economies. The opportunity is a potential growth in customer demand. Because of lower labor costs and the possibility to leapfrog to new technologies, GHG emissions reduction tends to be less expensive in developing countries. Companies operating in these settings may disproportionately benefit as favored suppliers to companies seeking to reduce the life-cycle emissions of their products. However, the risks are also important. Decarbonization investments may be costly and risky, and an underdeveloped carbon accounting infrastructure in developing countries may limit a firm's ability to monetize emissions reductions.

Scenarios

Decarbonization entails inherent risk. How will customer demand for climate-friendly products evolve? What climate-related risks will emerge? Which technologies will prove most efficient for decarbonizing production? And, critically, how will regulators support or hinder the transition? To manage amid these multiple dimensions of uncertainty, firms need to pursue decarbonization with a close eye to risk management. The risks are of two sorts: type 1 risks of getting too far ahead of technologies and markets; and type 2 risks of ignoring the reality of a decarbonized future and being left behind. The scale of these risks is potentially large. If your firm will have to provide low-carbon products or services in a decade, it needs to begin now to learn and innovate in order to compete in that future. Failure to plan for these new market conditions could threaten the very survival of the company.

One of the best approaches to managing multidimensional risk of this sort is through climate response scenario (CRS) planning. By gaming out specific scenarios, managers of different business units can piece together likely responses and outcomes. These scenarios help to identify opportunities and risks, while also educating managers across the firm about likely green targets and trajectories and the technologies that might be deployed to achieve them. CRSs can be especially helpful as a means for boards of directors to set a company's longer-term strategic objectives. They can help tease out firm-level and sector-level dynamics under different scientific and business assumptions. As with other scenario planning exercises, an external scenario planner or facilitator can increase the impact of this approach.

Organization

One of the surprises of our approach to addressing legacy fossil fuel industries like steel and chemicals is that some of our dominant legacy producers are also at the front end of decarbonization. In order for this sort of transformation to succeed, these legacy firms are having to reinvent fundamental industrial processes within existing corporate structures that have historically been optimized to operate in highly efficient ways in intensely competitive sectors. These organizations are fine-tuned to minimize risk, lower cost, and outcompete similarly organized firms. Yet the challenging work of decarbonization is going to require innovation, risk-taking, collaboration with competitors and regulators, and a huge new investment in novel technologies. To enable this sort of change, existing organizations will have to transform. This sort of cultural transformation requires difficult, often disruptive changes in organizational practice that extend deep into operational functions.

For incumbent firms with organizational structures optimized for efficiency, innovating to decarbonize can impose significant stresses. Suddenly, executives need to reorganize in ways that support experimentation and learning. One of the greatest challenges CEOs face as they move their firm down a net-zero pathway is resistance from managers who are often the point of the spear of decarbonization. How do business leaders overcome this sort of rigidity?

These are complex and challenging issues that we will touch on only very briefly. In general, though, we observe three main tools for creating a work environment that is optimized for the kind of exploration and risk-taking that the green energy transition will require.

- Emissions-aligned compensation

- Matrix organization

- Culture change

One approach is to link compensation to green outcomes. This important tool aligns the interests of senior management with stated emissions goals. But such schemes rarely extend to those operational managers who are key to finding and adopting new technologies. A second, complementary solution is to break up the organizational silos that have traditionally concentrated operational expertise where it was needed. When the Italian energy company Enel opted to embrace a fully green business strategy, for example, it also moved to a matrix organization structure in which managers reported both to their regional HQs and also to a functional supervisor. With

20   A CONCISE BUSINESS GUIDE TO CLIMATE CHANGE

dual reporting, managers shared more information and took greater risks.

The third and most challenging approach to induce the necessary change is through a project to rewrite the organization's cultural DNA. This sort of effort requires protracted emphasis on innovation and an acceptance or even celebration of failure. Because it applies to the entire organization, it must always be led from the top. Some of the most effective CEOs at the forefront of sectoral decarbonization have become change agents within their firms and sectors.

One of the obstacles to overcoming internal organizational challenges to decarbonization is that opposition may be rooted in part in climate denialism. Workers and managers may not be willing to express their views publicly, but some may not believe in the problem management is trying to solve. Climate denialism can have many sources: personal religious beliefs, misinformation from traditional and new social media, worry that a response to climate change may threaten their livelihoods. This sort of misinformation can be hard to overcome, and managers need to address the problem thoughtfully and with compassion. Two approaches can be effective. The first is to focus on firm-specific operational challenges of decarbonization, rather than the global climate crisis. Studies have shown that building a sense of agency, emphasizing the concrete actions that need to be taken, can reduce climate denialism. A second approach is to ensure that a climate response does not create a culture of fear. If your organization is going to eliminate jobs, then employees need to see that it will create other jobs, and that management is committed to transitioning their skills to these new areas.

External Organization

When firms set out on their decarbonization trajectory, they do not, indeed must not, travel alone. The new investments and technical standards that will be necessary to developing new processes and products will require intensive coordination, both up and down supply chains, and across competing firms. These firms need to spend more time coordinating with these external actors. Suppliers require clear commitments about carbon accounting and investments in GHG emissions reductions. As mentioned earlier, the large investments that suppliers have to make in order to decarbonize may require that buyers commit to longer-term contracts or offtake agreements that give them confidence. Offtake agreements also provide collateral to raise the necessary capital to finance these projects. Looking downstream, firms need to coordinate with customers around carbon emissions accounting standards and on the terms for which investments in carbon emissions reductions will be compensated. For example, can they expect a carbon premium?

Decarbonizing also commonly requires the drafting of sector-specific standards that firms negotiate in collaborative settings. In many cases, this requires that firms cooperate with their traditional competitors more than they are accustomed to. This kind of cozy rivalry, often referred to as "coopetition," allows firms to hold down the cost of decarbonizing by sharing risks and learning from the experiments of competitors. In some cases, existing industry associations can provide a platform for this kind of coordination. Where these do not exist, or where differences in firm interests make it impossible to use existing associations as a coordination point, new bodies may have to be created.

Finally, firms executing net-zero plans are increasingly engaging with nongovernmental groups that can provide both feedback and legitimacy through the process. Because many of the leaders in decarbonization have their roots as traditional energy, engineering, or consumer products firms that are seen as part of the problem, it can be hard to build the public's trust that they are now committed to emissions reduction. Their challenge is accentuated by the fact that some companies *are* simply engaging in climate window dressing rather than really reducing emissions. Increasingly, environmental NGOs are willing to partner with firms to monitor emissions and, when necessary, defend against accusations of green washing. They can also add their voice to the regulatory process, endorsing and legitimating new sectoral norms or processes that reduce emissions or increase sequestration. In the case of Golden Agri-Resources, mentioned earlier, the World Wildlife Fund and the Forest Stewardship Council are both working with the company to build public trust in their climate initiatives.

Leadership

Executing a corporate decarbonization strategy places extraordinary demands on a firm's CEO and leadership team. Decarbonization affects an entire organization, but it is led from the top. This means that the CEO must be the primary driver of the transition. Advocacy and high-level decisions cannot be handed off to an environmental, social, and governance (ESG) group or sustainability committee, although they will provide critical technical input. A firm's climate change response is a project that the top leadership must embrace and own.

In some cases, the corporate board may decide that a focus on decarbonization also requires new leadership. Such a decision can amplify the leadership challenge. In these cases, a new CEO may be brought in from the outside specifically to set a strong climate direction for the firm. As an outsider, they must quickly build confidence within their leadership team, with investors, and with customers. They must also instill confidence and purpose in lower-level managers who are often point persons for the operational changes necessary to reduce GHG emissions. The challenges of decarbonization for top management are great, but the potential rewards are commensurate. Leaders who successfully navigate the decarbonization project can have extraordinary impact. In an area in which leadership quality is essential, those who master the challenges will also be richly rewarded.

One of the key goals of the climate leader is to manage organizational uncertainty. The challenge is that CEOs who set net-zero targets for their firms are almost always committing to goals that they do not yet know how to achieve. A net-zero target for 2040 or 2050 typically exceeds conventional corporate planning horizons. It may also not yet be clear how to overcome particular technical hurdles. In addition, CEOs are increasingly being asked to sign off on carbon emission accounting data in which they may not have the highest level of confidence, since our tools and standards for assessing those emissions remain, to put it kindly, a work in progress. (See the following section on accounting.)

Successful CEOs are able to counter the risk and uncertainty that is inherent to a corporate green transition with a clear vision of the future stakes. They must articulate, and continuously reiterate, the case that GHG emissions reduction is critical to the future success and profitability of their firm. While this message may be embedded in a broader sense of societal and environmental responsibility, transformative CEOs focus on the impact on a firm's future competitive stance.

Second, corporate climate leaders need to build trust that they will be a consistent advocate and partner in the decarbonization project. This trust matters both within their organization and outside of it. Internally, managers who are asked to undertake risky organizational and technological innovations need to trust that their leaders will support them even in case of failure. Externally, partner businesses have to make their own investments to support the decarbonization project, but those investments depend on coordination.

24   A CONCISE BUSINESS GUIDE TO CLIMATE CHANGE

Can your firm be trusted? Will it remain steady? Leaders who are consistent and persistent in communicating their firm's approach to addressing climate change give confidence to partners that their climate targets are more than mere show.

Accounting

At the heart of the project of managing GHG emissions is the need to measure those emissions accurately and set targets for their reduction. Carbon accounting metrics provide transparency to external stakeholders, including investors and consumers, and allow firms to track and manage carbon emissions in order to meet internal goals. Increasingly, regulators are requiring that publicly traded companies disclose their GHG emissions. As they do so, these accounting standards are likely to evolve.

The world of climate accounting is one of daunting technical detail and proliferating standards and acronyms. Fortunately, all of the major accounting firms have built expertise in this area and are ready to provide carbon accounting services to their clients. Nonetheless, managers should be aware of the different disclosure standards that exist, as some provide better fit with their overall climate strategy. This is also an evolving area of accounting, so standards will change and, ideally, converge over time.

Disclosure

For the moment, there are nine major global standards for environmental reporting that address GHG emissions, as summarized in table 2-1. Some, like the Carbon Disclosure Project (CDP), focus narrowly on GHG emissions. Others, like the Global Reporting Initiative (GRI) and the UN Sustainable Development Goals (UN SDGs),

TABLE 2-1

Popular climate disclosure standards

Standard		Focus
CDP	Carbon Disclosure Project	Climate disclosure with a broad audience including regulators and the general public
CDSB	Climate Disclosure Standards Board	Climate-specific disclosure focused on investors
CSRD	Corporate Sustainability Reporting Directive	A mandatory European disclosure including climate and social impact
GRI	Global Reporting Initiative	A broad sustainability reporting standard that includes climate as well as other dimensions of corporate social responsibility
IFRS	International Financial Reporting Standards	A broad financial disclosure standard that includes climate outcomes
IR	Integrated Reporting Framework	A broad reporting format focused on investors that includes climate targets and outcomes
SASB	Sustainability Accounting Standards Board	General sustainability disclosure focused on investors
TCFD	Task Force on Climate-Related Financial Disclosures	Disclosures focusing on climate metrics and governance for use primarily by the financial sector
UN SDGs	United Nations Sustainable Development Goals	A broad sustainability reporting standard that aligns with the UN's 2030 sustainable development goals

include climate among a broader set of ESG categories. Also, some disclosure standards are intended primarily to allow investors to assess a firm's climate-related risk. The Task Force on Climate-Related Financial Disclosures, the International Sustainability Standards Board, and the Sustainability Accounting Standards Board all target primarily investors. The CDP and GRI, by contrast, are addressed to multiple stakeholders, including consumers and the broader public.

Many of these standards have been created as collaborations among different accounting or activist organizations. The earliest of them, the GRI, was jointly created in 1997 by the Coalition for Environmentally Responsible Economies, the Tellus Institute, and

26   A CONCISE BUSINESS GUIDE TO CLIMATE CHANGE

the UN Environment Programme. In 2013, GRI joined with the International Federation of Accountants and the Prince of Wales's Accounting for Sustainability Project to create the Integrated Reporting Framework overseen by the International Integrated Reporting Council. In 2017, GRI joined with the World Economic Forum's International Business Council and the UN Global Compact to support the UN SDGs as a standard for corporate ESG reporting. More recently, national governments have begun to set their own climate disclosure requirements and standards. In the European Union, for example, the Corporate Sustainability Reporting Directive (CSRD) imposes mandatory climate disclosure on a wide range of companies.

Even where not required by law, many corporations opt to disclose their climate impact by meeting several or even all of these accounting standards. Microsoft, for example, a leader in decarbonizing its business, reports metrics based on nearly all of the major ESG and climate disclosure standards. Companies that plan to be more selective will want to decide whether to focus narrowly on GHG emissions or on broader ESG reporting. They will also have to decide whether to emphasize disclosure targeted at investors, or ones that are geared toward a broader range of stakeholders. They should make such decisions in the context of their strategic assessment and its implications for their approach to climate change.

The diversity of corporate climate disclosure standards poses a special challenge for investors as they seek to assess their climate-related portfolio risk. Increasingly, doing so effectively requires distinguishing between firms that are making smart strategic investments to position themselves for the green transition, and those that are engaged primarily in deceptive marketing that hides inaction. Greenwashing poses an important challenge to firms that are committed to effective decarbonization, and investors stand on the front line of the struggle against this sort of deception. Effective monitoring and discipline by investors help to support those firms that are making real investments in decarbonization.

Setting Targets

Regardless of which of these climate reporting schemes a company chooses, two additional decisions will determine the broader framework for its climate reporting. The first calls on companies to declare *what* they are going to count when they report their carbon footprint. Should they include GHG emissions of suppliers, for example, or emissions resulting from the use of their products? In 1998, the World Resources Institute and World Business Council for Sustainable Development came together to create the Greenhouse Gas (GHG) Protocol to address such questions. The GHG Protocol framework defines three potential strategies, called "scopes," for setting emission targets. Scope 1 is the narrowest, including only the operations of the company, while omitting any energy sources it uses. Scope 2 adds to that the emissions from fossil fuels it burns to produce energy. Scope 3 is much more expansive, including emissions related both to upstream suppliers and to downstream use of products. The largest share of emissions embodied in many products is likely to derive from Scope 3. Decisions about whether to include Scope 3 emissions in a corporate decarbonization plan depend on a range of considerations, including the ease of Scope 3 abatement and the transparency of supply chains.

The second decision concerns the kind of goals corporations set for future GHG emissions. How ambitious should the goals be? Should they set absolute GHG reduction targets or emphasize greater GHG efficiency? Can they meet their targets by purchasing carbon offsets? To provide clarity around how corporations set and meet emissions targets, four groups came together in 2015 to found the

Science Based Targets initiative (SBTi).[7] The idea of the SBTi was to encourage and support corporations in pursuing emissions reductions targets that aligned with the climate goal set in the Paris Agreement. In 2021, SBTi launched a net-zero standard for firms. As its name suggests, this standard established guidelines for any firm setting a net-zero target. It called for a net-zero target date at or before 2050, a near-term target between five and ten years in the future, and a 10 percent cap on the share of emissions reductions that may be achieved through purchasing of offsets. All of these guidelines aligned closely with national decarbonization trajectories committed to under the Paris Agreement. And, unlike the wide range of GHG disclosure standards, the SBTi has emerged as an industrywide standard bearer.

Marginal Abatement Cost

Most firms will confront one last area of carbon accounting, which quantifies the cost of emissions reductions for different abatement activities. For any company or factory, some investments in abatement will generate positive financial returns—through either reduced energy use or productivity-enhancing innovations—while others will have negative returns and, hence, be costly. A marginal abatement cost curve (MACC) is a graph that presents all of the available abatement options, with the abatement cost of each option plotted on the vertical axis, and resulting emissions reduction on the horizontal access. MACCs typically list the least-cost abatement options on the left, moving toward the most expensive costs on the right. At the very left, the lowest-cost abatement efforts typically generate a positive return. A common example of this is switching from incandescent to LED or natural lighting. On the far right are the most expensive abatement projects, including investments in new production technologies and worker retraining.

MACCs, the bread and butter of climate consulting services, provide a useful overview of what a decarbonization pathway might look like. Yet, as with all accounting schemes, insights from a MACC are only one element in a broader strategic approach to decarbonization. In the past, it often made sense for firms to begin with items on the far left, for example, then work their way to the right. This should, in theory, offer the least-cost pathway to decarbonization. MACCs are, however, only a tool, and managers should keep in mind the broader sectoral dynamics of the green transition as it emerges.

One limitation, for example, is that the cost of decarbonization technologies is changing quickly. Whereas solar photovoltaic would have looked like a very expensive decarbonization option a decade ago and, hence, be positioned on the right side of the MACC, today in many sunny geographies the installation of solar photovoltaic panels represents a source of cost reduction that places it on the far left. And there are signs that other decarbonization technologies, such as batteries and bioreactors, are undergoing similar price shifts. A second consideration relates to the strategic logic of the green transition for any given sector. It may make sense, for example, for companies to prioritize expensive investments that appear on the right side of the MACC in order to become a technology and market leader through the transition. Firms that focus only on left-side abatement investments may miss a broader sectoral transformation that is under way.

Regulation

Businesses are not accustomed to treating regulators as potential allies as they innovate. Historically, the regulator-firm relationship has been tense and frequently confrontational. Yet in a time when many national governments have begun to see climate technologies as the focus of national industrial policies, firms are increasingly finding that the tone of their interactions with government agencies is changing. In part, national regulatory agencies are increasingly being tasked with providing financial subsidies to firms investing in climate technologies. They also are trying to draft new climate-friendly regulations, and to do so in ways that support and de-risk the climate investments that domestic firms are making. In the United States, companies pursuing subsidies through the Inflation Reduction Act have hired lobbying firms to help build political support for their applications. In Europe, negotiations over the details of how the CBAM is being deployed have allowed European green industry leaders to have a say in implementation. In all cases, CEOs report intensified communications with regulatory agencies about the design of new climate policies. In many cases, investment decisions hinge critically on regulatory support, and ongoing communications with regulators can provide access to, and some degree of influence over, that regulatory context.

While these kinds of interactions with regulators may feel uncomfortable or unfamiliar for many firms, they play a growing role in de-risking new climate investments. In general, regulators can provide three kinds of supports for firms leaning into climate mitigation. First, climate responses can be capital intensive, and government subsidies can help to make risky new technologies profitable. Second, government agencies can write regulation that puts a hand on the economic scale to favor decarbonization. This may take the form of higher emissions standards—as, for example, in the auto industry—or a sectoral tax on carbon. Third, governments can support fundamental research to unlock entire supply chains. For example, governments in Europe, the United States, and Japan are all subsidizing critical green hydrogen technologies in the hope that this may provide an alternative to fossil-fuel-based hydrocarbon fuels.

Firms have a number of options for approaching regulators. Large firms may reach out directly to talk with agencies governing their sector. They are also increasingly receiving incoming calls asking for input or guidance. Often the CEO is the point-person in these kinds of government connections. Short of that, however, firms may rely on existing or new industry associations in order to interact with regulators and lawmakers. Associational representation can provide a powerful consensus view of a sector that will have more impact on regulators. US insurance companies, for example, have formed a Net-Zero Insurance Alliance to help advocate for new strategies to manage climate-related insurance risk. In Europe, the competition authority has been explicitly instructed to allow such sectoral coordination around climate adaptation. In other sectors, regulators may become the nexus of debate between incumbent firms and green challengers. Climate-friendly green steel producers in Europe, for example, are at odds with incumbent steel producers over the phaseout of free carbon emissions allocations. Ultimately, the outcome in such contests will lean toward those who have a voice in the decision. Hence, whether working collectively or alone, firms will increasingly need to engage with regulators over new rules and supports that go to the heart of their business strategy and production technology.

One complexity around regulation is the uncertainty introduced by political partisanship with respect to climate change. Especially in jurisdictions where no political consensus exists around decarbonization—the United States is the most extreme case—changes in political control can lead to large swings in public policy. Firms can manage this sort of political risk in two ways. First, relationships with regulators should be treated as long-term investments, not one-off interventions. As unfamiliar as it sounds, effective lobbying efforts will require trust between firms and agencies, and that sort of trust must be built over time. While political support for decarbonization will inevitably wax and wane, firms need to focus on the longer term. Second, state and local regulators can be valuable partners in negotiations at the national and regional

32   A CONCISE BUSINESS GUIDE TO CLIMATE CHANGE

levels. Not all regulators are aligned, and a powerful local ally can help to influence state and national policies.

Concluding Thoughts

It should be clear that the SOLAR framework provides more of a decision matrix than an absolute prescription for how firms should approach decarbonization. It emphasizes three features of the transition that may require that firms change how they think about climate change.

First, climate change has become a bottom-line issue for companies, linked to planning around investment and innovation and with implications for future profitability. If boards of directors and top management are not thinking about climate in view of their medium-term and longer-term profitability, they are probably not thinking about it productively. That does not necessarily mean that they should act aggressively. It may be that a strategic assessment leads to a conclusion to take a wait-and-see approach. But leaders must make such decisions based on a broader strategic assessment. And they must remember that the risks of inaction may be as significant as the risks of climate action.

Second, our climate transition is being led as much by older incumbent firms as by new technology startups. To navigate this transition effectively, existing chemicals and manufacturing firms, for example, are having to reorganize and reinvent themselves in order to support and embrace greater flexibility and risk-taking. Success in this sort of reorganization leans heavily on the leadership skills of executives. This implies that effective leaders may reap significant dividends through the climate transition.

Third, successful firms are increasingly aligning their own investment strategies with the economic goals of the countries or regions in which they operate. In order to meet their national decarbonization targets, governments must rely on and support firms that are leading this process. In turn, firms that are decarbonizing are receiving increasing supports and protections from national governments that actively support their success. Conversely, firms that pursue strategies that contradict national and regional economic goals may increasingly face regulatory headwinds.

CHAPTER 3

CLIMATE SCIENCE

This chapter introduces the physical drivers of climate change and their impact. It presents the basic science that connects carbon dioxide and methane emissions to shifting temperature and weather patterns as global temperatures rise. By the end, the reader will be able to answer some of the hard questions that relate increases in greenhouse gases to changes in regional weather conditions. For example, why are some regions beginning to experience greater aridity caused by climate change, while others are suffering from more intense rains and inundation? Why are hurricanes predicted to become stronger? Why is the level of the sea rising? We answer these questions by exploring the models scientists use to explain what is happening to our climate today and to make predictions about the future.

But first, why focus on the science? With other technical phenomena, we don't typically feel the need to understand the underlying mechanisms in order to confront the business challenges and opportunities they create. The statistical technology behind large language models, for example, will remain beyond the comprehension of most of its users. That will not stop entrepreneurs from discovering new and productive applications of the technology. Nor do most business leaders need to spend time studying the workings of the internet, or blockchain, or deep learning algorithms. For most disruptive technologies, we take the technology as given and focus on its real-world possibilities.

Climate change is different. Business executives at all levels of leadership need to have a reasonably good grasp of the chemistry and physics behind climate change. As they confront the challenges of corporate decarbonization, executives will rely primarily on technical experts to conduct the detailed work of emissions accounting and project scoping. They may be working with consulting firms to design marginal abatement cost curves, with risk managers to consider climate adaptation measures, or with financial advisors to design green finance instruments. To communicate effectively with these support providers, executives need to be comfortable speaking the same language they do, and that language is anchored in the basic physics of climate change. Fortunately, most of the relevant science was discovered in the nineteenth century and is at the level typically covered in introductory college-level science classes. What executives need to know is not, in other words, overly complex.

Unfortunately, there is a second and more important reason that a basic familiarity with the science of climate change is important, and it is primarily defensive. At a moment when debates about climate change and our response to it are politically and economically fraught, a basic level of knowledge offers a necessary layer of protection. It is often observed that a little knowledge can be a dangerous thing—in this case, the opposite is true. Even a basic grounding in climate science can insulate you from a surprisingly large body of misinformation that circulates on the internet, across social media platforms, and even (although less over time) in the established media. Our goal in this chapter is to help you distinguish science-based propositions from those that are fictional. Like a magnetic compass for a traveler, a familiarity with climate science will not tell you what your destination should be, nor by what conveyance you should travel, but it can help you keep your bearings and ensure you are moving in the direction of your choice.

Climate Modeling

What we refer to as a climate model is actually three separate kinds of model that we combine in order to predict what will happen to our weather in the future. I think of them as a three-layer cake. The bottommost layer—the foundation of the rest—is called an energy balance model (EBM). This class of model measures how much solar radiation heats the surface of the Earth, and how much energy the Earth radiates back into space. When incoming radiation exceeds outgoing, the surface temperature of the Earth rises. Relatively small differences between incoming and outgoing radiation have led to 1.2°C average global warming over the past 150 years.

The second layer is called a general circulation model (GCM). GCMs describe what happens to the major Earth systems as the surface warms. Most solar radiation falls on the lower latitudes of the Earth, in the temperate and tropical zones close to the equator. The polar regions receive solar radiation at a very low angle, limiting the amount of energy absorbed. The resulting temperature gradient induces flows of air and water that shunt tropical heat toward the cooler poles. The resulting pattern of circulation of air and water drives the major weather conditions we observe on Earth. GCMs describe these flows.

The top layer of our cake is a model of human response to the resulting climate. To predict our likely response to different degrees

38 A CONCISE BUSINESS GUIDE TO CLIMATE CHANGE

of climate change, social scientists engage in a sort of scenario analysis, laying out alternative possible futures by combining the geophysics of climate systems with likely human responses to them. These models are called integrated assessment models (IAMs) because they combine future economic and climate scenarios. Researchers use IAMs to imagine what the Earth is likely to look like ten, fifty, or a hundred years from now. This class of model also provides the basis for predicting the future economic cost of climate change. We address these economic projections and their implications in chapter 4.

The Energy Balance Model

All warm bodies emit energy in the form of electromagnetic radiation. The warmer they are, the higher the frequency of radiation they emit. The Sun, at around 5,800°C, emits radiation mostly in the visible and infrared part of the electromagnetic spectrum.[1] On Earth, we perceive this radiation as visible light and an invisible warming of the skin. The Earth is of course colder than the Sun, averaging roughly 27°C. It emits energy at much lower frequencies that are invisible to the human eye, in the infrared range (see figure 3-1). Infrared emissions have longer wavelengths than visible light, but shorter than radio waves. In the absence of an external perturbation, or forcing, all of the solar radiation absorbed by the Earth from the Sun is re-emitted back into space at longer wavelengths, keeping the Earth's energy in balance.

Not all energy emitted from the Sun is absorbed by the Earth, nor does all energy emitted by the Earth escape directly into space. About a quarter of all solar radiation hitting the Earth's atmosphere is reflected back into space by clouds or light-colored surfaces like snow and ice. The degree of reflectivity of these surfaces

CLIMATE SCIENCE

FIGURE 3-1

Solar and earth radiation with greenhouse gas absorption spectra

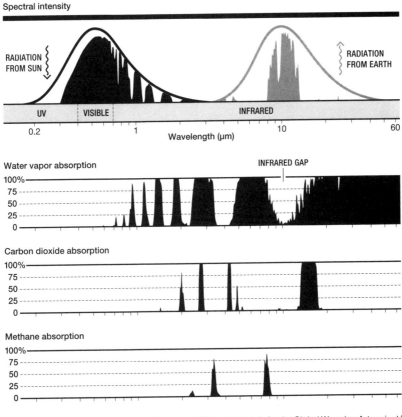

Source: Wikkiwonkk, based on the original work of Robert A. Rohde for the Global Warming Art project/Wikimedia Commons/public domain.

is called albedo. Albedo is measured as a percentage, from 0 percent to 100 percent, with higher albedo indicating greater reflectivity. High albedo is one of the reasons that the polar ice pack helps to keep the Earth cool. As the ice melts, darker waters with lower albedo reflect less solar radiation, causing the Earth to warm. The extent to which global warming will alter Earth's cloud cover, and therefore its albedo, is a challenging scientific question that remains the focus of intensive research.

Earth emits energy back into space at lower frequencies, in the infrared range of the electromagnetic spectrum. Not all of the emitted energy escapes right away. The reason has to do with the way these low-frequency electromagnetic waves interact with the atmosphere. The warming effect from this interaction is what we call the greenhouse effect.

The atmosphere is made up of gas molecules, including nitrogen, oxygen, carbon dioxide, methane, and water vapor. All have characteristic frequencies at which they oscillate, called their resonant frequencies. When infrared energy emitted by Earth matches the resonant frequency of these gas molecules, the molecules vibrate sympathetically, absorbing some of the energy. As they are excited, they become warmer, and in turn reemit that heat into the surrounding atmosphere. As the atmosphere warms, it reemits infrared radiation back toward the Earth, creating a sort of blanket that traps the heat below it. This is the greenhouse effect, and without it the Earth would be a cold, hostile environment.

Of the gas molecules in the atmosphere, gaseous water absorbs energy over the broadest spectrum of infrared frequencies and accounts for the largest share (58 percent) of heat-trapping greenhouse effect on Earth. However, water does not absorb energy across the whole range of infrared frequencies the Earth emits (see figure 3-1). Instead, the range of frequencies that coincides with the peak of Earth's infrared radiation are *not* absorbed by gaseous water in the atmosphere. This part of the electromagnetic spectrum is called the infrared gap. It is through the infrared gap that much of Earth's emitted radiation escapes. By allowing infrared radiation to escape, this gap keeps the Earth's temperature from building up too high. It is within the infrared gap that CO_2, CH_4, and N_2O play their starring roles. That is because each happens to absorb infrared radiation at frequencies that fall within the gap. (Other abundant atmospheric compounds, like oxygen and nitrogen, do not vibrate at these

CLIMATE SCIENCE

frequencies and, hence, do not block Earth's emissions.) Of the major greenhouse gases, CO_2 has the greatest impact after water vapor, absorbing and reemitting 26 percent of infrared radiation emitted from the surface of the Earth. Methane is next, at 11 percent. As the share of carbon dioxide and methane in the atmosphere increases, they increasingly occlude the infrared gap. Like lowering the blinds on a window, the space for emitted infrared radiation to escape the Earth is reduced.

The entire Earth absorbs 120 petawatts (quadrillion watts) of solar energy as visible and infrared radiation. That number serves as a reminder of how powerful the Sun is. By comparison, all of human civilization today uses only about 0.015 petawatts of power. Because a petawatt is an unwieldy measure, climate scientists instead focus on the average solar radiation that hits a square meter of the Earth's surface, measured as W/m^2 (watts per square meter). The resulting flow of energy is called radiant flux, and it describes how much solar energy is absorbed by the Earth, and how much the Earth re-emits back into space.

Beginning in the early 1990s, NASA began launching a series of orbital sensors to detect the rate of radiative energy flow into and out of Earth's atmosphere. The project was called the Clouds and Earth Radiant Energy System (CERES), and it has provided increasingly accurate measures of Earth's radiant flux. CERES measurements show that the surface of the Earth has been absorbing an average of 240.5 W/m^2 in the visible and infrared spectrum. The Earth has in turn been re-radiating longer wavelength infrared energy at an average of 239.9 W/m^2. That means that *almost* all of the energy absorbed by the Earth is being re-radiated—but not all. That little excess, amounting to 0.6 W/m^2, is the source of rising global temperatures. CERES has also found that our radiative surplus has grown over time, from an average of 0.5 W/m^2 from 2005 to 2010, to an average of 0.9 W/m^2 from 2015 to 2020.

Of the cumulative energy that the Earth has absorbed over the past century and a half of fossil fuel extraction and burning, over 90 percent so far has been absorbed by the oceans. Water has an unusually strong ability to absorb energy without a large rise in temperature. This property, called heat capacity, has meant that the impact of our global energy surplus on air and surface temperatures over the past several decades has been muted by the absorptive sink of the world's oceans. The heat absorbed in the oceans has temporarily sheltered us from the full impact of climate change. Scientists call this sort of time lag thermal inertia.

Unfortunately, thermal inertia also works in the other direction. Even if we were to eliminate all GHG emissions today, it might take several decades and up to a century for surface temperatures to stabilize. The global average surface temperature of the Earth, averaged over the past five years, is 1.2°C (2.2°F) above its preindustrial level. Even in a hard-stop scenario, the effect of thermal inertia implies that we are probably already committed to an eventual temperature rise of over 2.3°C (4.1°F).[2] Realistic GHG emission adjustment pathways imply significantly higher end-point temperatures.

The General Circulation Model

Energy balance models deal with the *average* radiative flows onto and away from the Earth's surface. Those flows in turn determine the average global surface temperature. In practice, of course, more solar energy is absorbed at the equator than on the Earth's poles. Tropical lands bake under intense year-round light. At high latitudes, even summer sunlight hits the ground at a low angle, reducing how much solar radiation warms any given area of land.

The situation is very different for the infrared radiation emitted by the Earth. Since even the Arctic is warm relative to the cold

FIGURE 3-2

Earth energy balance by latitude

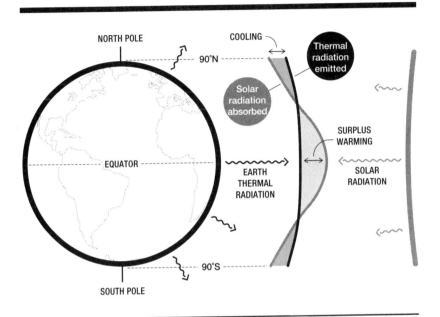

of space, both the equator and the Arctic emit a lot of electromagnetic radiation. While the warmer tropical zone emits somewhat more than the colder Arctic, the intensity of outgoing radiation is less dependent on latitude than is the intensity of incoming solar radiation. That means that while the Earth's equatorial zone experiences a large energy surplus, absorbing solar radiation that exceeds its infrared emissions, the poles of the Earth are in continuous energy deficit (see figure 3-2). Like a freezer, the Arctic is being continuously cooled, which raises a key problem. What keeps the poles from getting ever colder and the equator from getting ever warmer?

This temperature gradient is the primary driver of the Earth's main water currents and atmospheric air flows. These flows shunt heat that builds up at the equator north and south toward the Earth's poles. The resulting circulation flows, in the form of ocean currents and atmospheric winds, dictate most of the important regional weather patterns of the Earth.

General circulation models attempt to describe these flows. They use equations built to characterize fluids to model movements of air and water on a global scale. These equations are well understood because they are also used to model the performance of airplanes, cars, and boats. As one might imagine, these fluid dynamics models are computationally intensive. They tend to be run on some of the fastest supercomputers in the world. The increasing speed of those computers is helping to make the models more accurate.

As most of the energy surplus of the Earth is absorbed by the oceans, the most important conveyor of energy from the tropics to the poles takes place via ocean currents. Until recently, most of those currents have been hidden to us. Beginning in the early 2000s, researchers around the world collaborated to launch what is now a fleet of three thousand autonomous research buoys that constitute the Argo program. As they float around the world's oceans, they periodically dive deep under the sea and then return to the surface, while also measuring water temperature, salinity, and other features. Argo allowed us to detect the primary underwater river that shunts heat from the equator toward the Arctic. That current is called the thermohaline circulation. The name refers to the fact that differences in water temperature (thermo) and salinity (haline) drive the flow.

The main engine for the global thermohaline circulation is in the North Atlantic, where a massive warm ocean current flows up the East Coast of the United States and Canada and into the Labrador and Greenland seas. Once in the Arctic, the flow begins to cool. Cool water is denser than warm water, and the flow of water sinks a mile down into the depths of the Arctic Ocean. From there, it starts a long, deep journey back toward the equator and on into the South Atlantic Ocean. This north-south oceanic river is called the Atlantic Meridional Overturning Circulation (AMOC), and its flow keeps

CLIMATE SCIENCE   **45**

northern Europe warm, while also determining the temperature and rate of ice formation of the Arctic Ocean. While this circulation does not move very fast—about walking pace—it transports a volume of water equal to fifteen times the discharge of all the rivers on Earth.[3] If this massive flow were to slow or stop, as some climate scientists have warned, Europe and the Arctic would become significantly colder.

The global energy imbalance between the equator and the poles also drives the major air currents of the Earth. Those currents in turn create most of our regional weather patterns. To see how, we need to introduce two basic physical principles that govern the ways in which fluids (in this case, air) flow. They are convection and the Coriolis effect.

Convection

One of the most important geophysical principles governing flows of air or water is called convection. To understand convection, a home kitchen example will be illustrative. When you place a pot of water on the stove to boil, the water at the bottom of the pot warms more than the water at the top. As warming water expands, it seeks to rise to the surface, allowing cooler, denser water to sink to the bottom. But how does the rising warm water find its way past the sinking cold water? The answer—which you can see if you boil a pot of loose tea—is that the hot water tends to move across the bottom of the pot until it gathers into an area where a chimney of hot water is rising. At the surface, colder water also moves sideways until it finds a column of cold water sinking to the bottom. This set of flows, taken together, generates a circular vertical flow that is called a convection cell.

The same phenomenon occurs in the Earth's atmosphere, though at a much larger scale. At the equator, where high surface temperatures heat the air, that air rises upward. Once it reaches the upper atmosphere, it begins moving north and south away from the equator. It travels about two thousand miles at high altitude until, having cooled, it becomes denser and sinks back down to Earth. Meanwhile, air near the Earth's surface below flows *toward* the equator, in order to join the column of rising hot air there. This circular flow of air above the tropics is called the Hadley cell—named after the eighteenth-century British amateur meteorologist George Hadley, who first proposed that it existed. The Hadley cell occurs in both the Northern and Southern Hemispheres and extends from the equator to about 30° north and south latitude. In the Northern Hemisphere, that corresponds with the southern border of the United States, the southern shore of the Mediterranean Sea, and roughly the midline through China. In general, surface air below this line flows southward toward the equator.

At the Earth's poles, the opposite convection flow occurs. As cooling air over the poles becomes denser, it sinks toward the Earth's surface, pushing air on the surface toward the equator. As this surface flow warms, it begins to rise into the upper atmosphere again, at about 60° latitude. From there, it makes its high-altitude trek back to the North and South Poles. This is called the Arctic cell. In the Northern Hemisphere, it creates surface winds that draw cold air out of the Arctic and into the center of the North American and Asian continents. These flows can cause extraordinarily cold winter conditions in places like Montana, Siberia, and Mongolia.

Between the Hadley cells in the tropics and the Arctic cell at the North and South Poles, a third convection cell drives winds in the mid-latitude, temperate zones. This third convection cell, called the Ferrel cell, is squeezed between falling air from the Hadley cell and rising air from the Arctic cell. These two flows induce a reverse circulation that drives surface air northward across the middle latitudes of the Northern Hemisphere (see figure 3-3).

CLIMATE SCIENCE 47

FIGURE 3-3

Atmospheric convection cells

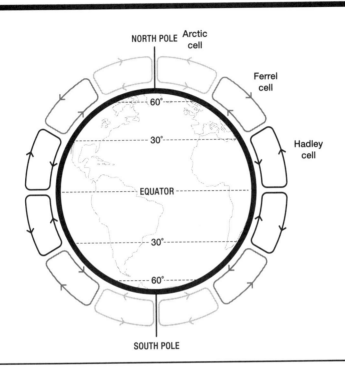

Ninety percent of the world's population lives between the equator and 60°N parallel. In this region, the Hadley and Ferrel cells cause surface winds below 30°N to blow southward and above 30°N to blow northward. And these surface winds, driven by atmospheric convection cells, have a critical impact on our weather.

The Coriolis Effect

To understand how these air flows create the weather we experience, however, we need to introduce one further physical phenomenon. It is the Coriolis effect, named for the nineteenth-century French mathematician who studied the forces that occur on rotating bodies.

He was mostly interested in water wheels, but the Earth also rotates, and so similar principles apply. The Coriolis effect is an extension of Isaac Newton's first law of motion applied to rotating bodies. The first law states that momentum in a physical system must be preserved.[4] It implies that if we throw a rock in space, it will keep going at the same speed in the same direction. Coriolis noted that something similar was true for objects on a revolving surface like the Earth.

To see what he had in mind, imagine a person on a carousel, sitting on the outermost horse. Each time the carousel makes a full rotation, she travels a certain distance. That distance is greater than the distance traveled by a rider sitting on a horse closer to the center. Because she is traveling further in the same amount of time, the outer rider has more momentum (called angular momentum). Now what happens if the outer rider decides to move to an inner horse while the ride is going? She gets off her horse and begins walking inward on the turning carousel. When she does so, however, she will end up *ahead* of the inner horse, since she still has the momentum build up by moving at a higher speed at the outer edge of the carousel. To get to the inner horse, she will have to shed that momentum, actively pushing herself to the left. (Really, try it, but be careful.)

This is a playground example, but the principle applies on the scale of the Earth. Seen from above the North Pole, the Earth turns counterclockwise. When winds flow northward from the equator toward the Arctic, they follow an increasingly shorter path through space, and like the carousel rider, they seem to turn to the right, driven by their greater momentum. Conversely, winds moving southward from the pole have insufficient momentum to match the speed at the equator. This causes them to appear to slow down, also turning to the right. This tendency of north-south winds in the Northern Hemisphere to turn to the right is what we call the Coriolis effect.

The rightward veer of north-south winds has had vital consequences for both weather and human civilization. Due to atmospheric convection, surface winds blow southward and northward from approximately the 30th parallel—a line that passes through roughly the center of the North Atlantic Ocean. As the northward-flowing surface winds of the Ferrel cell veer to the east, they drive the prevailing westerly winds that flow from North America toward Europe. In the tropics, off the west coast of North Africa, the southward-blowing surface winds of the Hadley cell turn toward the west, creating the easterly trade winds.

These wind patterns have dictated not only regional wind patterns, but also the main trade routes of early Atlantic traders. Because of the Coriolis effect, European sailing vessels had to sail south to the coast of Africa before they could catch winds that would take them to the Americas. The slave trade and the trade winds went hand in hand. Once in the Americas, and laden with tobacco and cotton, traders then had to travel north along the coast of the Eastern United States in order to catch the prevailing westerlies back to Europe.

Historical Climate Data

The general circulation models that simulate the flows of air and water on Earth take the output of the energy balance models and translate it into regional climates and even local weather. Some of the processes it simulates are complex. Critical processes like cloud formation, which affects how much solar radiation is reflected back into space, and plant transpiration, which contributes moisture to the air, all have to be modeled and incorporated into the GCM. In order to ensure the models are reflecting the real world, researchers spend a lot of computer time simulating past climatic conditions. Once they have tuned the models to explain climate patterns from

50   A CONCISE BUSINESS GUIDE TO CLIMATE CHANGE

the past, they can have more confidence that they will make useful predictions about the future. To do that, climate scientists need accurate historical climate data.

What we know about that past climate has been gleaned from many sources, such as tree rings and coral growth patterns, but two sources have been especially useful.[5] Ice cores provide one valuable historical measure. Taken from ancient ice pack in Greenland and Antarctica, these cores contain air bubbles that serve as time capsules from past ages. From those pockets of trapped air, we can measure the concentration of carbon dioxide. The crystal structure of the ice in the core also gives direct evidence of the temperature at the time it was formed. These ice cores provide us a continuous history of the Earth's temperature and atmospheric carbon dioxide concentration going back almost one million years.

A second important source of historical climate data comes from the dead remains of tiny marine plankton called foraminifera (forams). These marine plankton form shells, called tests, for which the exact molecular composition provides evidence of the temperature and acidity of the water at the time they were living. For example, as the temperature of the water in which they live increases, a higher share of the element magnesium replaces calcium in the foram tests. That ratio can be detected and measured many millennia later. Fortunately, forams sink to the bottom of the sea when they die, leaving a layered record of the historical climate conditions in which they lived. Using cores from the bottom of the seas, researchers have been able to reconstruct a history of ocean surface temperatures that goes back many millions of years.

Data from ice cores and foram tests, along with other sources, reveals dramatic historical fluctuations in the Earth's carbon dioxide and surface temperature. At the height of the last ice age, which lasted nearly 100,000 years, temperatures were nearly 10°C below our average temperature today. Vast volumes of water accumulated

CLIMATE SCIENCE 51

in terrestrial ice sheets during this time, lowering the ocean surface 120 meters (nearly 400 feet) below today's level. And that was only the most recent of a series of ice ages that have occurred over the past million years. This history of past temperature fluctuations raises obvious questions about the rising temperatures today. Could we today be facing another, natural climate cycle?

Most of the computer time scientists spend running general circulation models focuses on these historical cycles of the climate. With their GCMs calibrated to replicate past climatic cycles, climate scientists can then run them forward in order to identify the distinctive impact that humans are having and will have on the climate. They can imagine an Earth without industrialization, without the extraction and burning of fossil fuels, without mass agriculture and the accompanying methane emissions.

When they do this, the result is clear. Without human emission of GHGs, the average global surface temperature would not be rising. There are about thirty different research groups running GCMs in the world, and all of them have found the same result. The rise in temperature we are experiencing today is caused by human GHG emissions.

When scientists run their climate models forward to try to understand what a future of climate change will look like, their outcomes become less certain. Parts of the process remain difficult to model accurately. Some natural systems involve strong feedback effects. When ice melts, for example, darker water absorbs more solar energy and leads to faster ice melt. Such positive feedback loops are hard to predict. Other sources of uncertainty involve tipping-point phenomena. The Thwaites Glacier in West Antarctica, for example, has become progressively destabilized, as the ice sheet that has been holding it back is breaking up. Should Thwaites start flowing faster, it could begin a process that might quickly raise global sea levels by two feet. When and under what circum-

52 A CONCISE BUSINESS GUIDE TO CLIMATE CHANGE

stances such a surge might occur is the focus of intensive field research, but currently hard to predict.

Integrated Assessment Models

By far the most challenging phenomenon to predict, however, is how humans are likely to respond to rising global temperatures. Will we act quickly and decisively to reduce future carbon emissions? Will we be sluggish or disorganized, leading to prolonged burning of fossil fuels? Answers to these questions are critical to understanding what Earth's future climate might look like. Rather than trying to answer them directly, a third kind of model attempts to explore a range of scenarios of human response. This is called the integrated assessment model (IAM), and as the name suggests, it integrates our geophysical climate models with economic and societal scenarios to paint a comprehensive picture of our future climate as it is affected by human activity.

While there are many different approaches to creating IAMs, most have three components. The first is a set of societal scenarios called shared socioeconomic pathways (SSPs). Beginning in the mid-1990s, the United Nation's Intergovernmental Panel on Climate Change (IPCC) convened a group of economists, demographers, and futurists to assess how human society was likely to evolve over the coming decades during which climate change would be felt. The assignment was impossibly hard, but also critically important to predicting what the world under climate change would look like. Their approach was to provide alternative potential narratives about the likely human evolution, including factors like population, GDP growth, and the degree of international cooperation. Critically, the SSPs addressed variables like population and fossil fuel use but did not try to predict exactly how humans were likely to respond to cli-

CLIMATE SCIENCE

mate change. In 2016, the group issued its first set of future climate narratives. They were incorporated for the first time into the IPCC's *Sixth Assessment Report*, published in 2021–2022.

The resulting scenarios described five different potential trajectories for society from today until 2100. These are labeled SSP1 to SSP5. They differ in their assumptions about our capacity to mitigate (slow) climate change, on the one hand, and to adapt to the effects of climate change on the other. The most optimistic scenario is SSP1, called "Sustainability—Taking the Green Road," in which we aggressively pursue both mitigation and adaptation. The worst-case scenario is SSP5, called the "Fossil-Fueled Development" path, in which we focus on adaptation and engage in relatively little mitigation. The mid-range scenario is SSP2, called the "Middle-of-the-Road" path. The IPCC emphasizes that SSP2 is not more likely than any of the others, but it is nonetheless commonly treated as an average scenario.

While work on the SSPs was occurring, a different group of researchers modeled the likely climate impacts of these scenarios on the climate. They assumed different possible GHG emissions scenarios and ran these through climate models to generate future warming trajectories that are referred to as representative concentration pathways (RCPs). There are seven standard RCPs used in the IPCC's *Sixth Assessment Report*. The different RCPs are defined in terms of their impact on the Earth's projected radiative balance in 2100. The most extreme of the scenarios, called RCP8.5, foresees radiative forcing due to greenhouse gases of 8.5 W/m^2 by the end of the century. In other words, the Earth in 2100 will be absorbing 8.5 W/m^2 more than it is emitting back into space. This extreme scenario leads to a rise in global average temperature of 5°C, and a one-meter increase in sea level. The most optimistic scenario, and the one that is compatible with the Paris Agreement's goal of capping global average temperature rise to 1.5°C, is called RCP1.9.

54   A CONCISE BUSINESS GUIDE TO CLIMATE CHANGE

A Note on SSPs and RCPs

One of the key goals of integrated assessment models (IAMs) is to link specific shared socioeconomic pathways (SSPs) to corresponding representative concentration pathways (RCPs). However, different IAMs can generate quite different outcomes. This means that depending on what IAM is employed, SSPs may lead to different scenarios with different RCP outcomes. The SSP1, for example, may lead to RCP1.9 or RCP2.6. In general, researchers tend to focus on three common scenarios: optimistic SSP1/RCP2.6, pessimistic SSP5/RCP8.5, and mid-range SSP2/RCP4.0.

In this scenario, the Earth's radiant energy surplus will top out at 1.9 W/m^2 in 2100, with sea-level rise of one-half meter (1.5 feet). See the sidebar "A Note on SSPs and RCPs" for more information.

Neither the SSP nor the RCP directly address how humans are likely to change their behaviors in response to the growing impact of climate change. To explore this last critical link, researchers rely on IAMs to translate each SSP scenario into future projected GHG emissions described by the RCPs. To do this, IAMs rely on complex economic simulations to project likely climate-related loss and human adaptation to it.[6] IAMs are highly varied in their conclusions. Research teams around the world have developed dozens of IAMs and have come to highly varied conclusions with quite different outcomes. This is unlike the EBMs and GCMs, for which different research teams have found very similar results. Policy makers commonly rely on more than one of these IAMs to make projections about the likely economic impact of proposed climate responses in the different scenarios.

The best-known IAM is the Dynamic Integrated Climate-Economy (DICE) model, developed by Nobel Prize–winning Yale economist William Nordhaus. DICE projects a relatively low future cost of climate change and has been criticized for prescribing a relatively unambitious response. Other models make different assumptions that lead to higher predicted costs from climate change. IAMs like DICE are used for a range of research purposes. Most importantly, they allow economists to assess the future economic cost of climate change. As discussed in chapter 4, cost-benefit calculations about future impacts play an important role in determining optimal carbon tax policy.

From Climate to Weather

While the three layers of modeling interact to describe our current and future climate, the challenges we confront with rising global temperatures will be experienced concretely as changing regional weather conditions. This most often manifests as intensification of existing weather phenomena: more powerful hurricanes, torrential rains, or extreme summer heat. Critically, however, weather will continue to fluctuate in familiar ways. We will have snap cold spells, winter blizzards, and rains that replenish evaporating reservoirs. As predictably as the arrival of spring, climate change skeptics will point to these kinds of weather events as evidence against a changing climate. Ignore them. What we know about climate change is that swings in weather conditions are likely to become more pronounced. Amid the daily fluctuating weather, however, longer-term patterns are increasingly emerging.

Two trends with widespread implications are growing regional patterns of deluge and aridity, and rising sea levels. The remainder of this chapter addresses the causes of these patterns.

One of the key impacts of a warming climate is that it allows the air to hold more moisture. For every 1°C in temperature rise, the air holds 7 percent more gaseous water. When moisture-laden winds

56   A CONCISE BUSINESS GUIDE TO CLIMATE CHANGE

bump into a cold air mass, that water vapor condenses, dumping the water as rain. With more moisture in the air, such rains can become deluges. Our climate models predict that rainfall will become more intense as the global temperature warms. Where that happens, however, depends on global wind patterns.

In the Northern Hemisphere, the winds that blow north from roughly the 30th parallel driven by the Ferrel cell are responsible for much of the hydrology and agricultural bounty established around major river systems. In the eastern United States, northbound winds draw moisture-laden warm air off the Gulf of Mexico to feed the Ohio and Mississippi rivers. Two-thirds of American agricultural output is grown along the drainage basins of these two rivers. In Europe, similar flows draw moist Mediterranean air into central Europe, where it feeds the Rhine and Danube rivers. In China, moist warm water from the South China Sea blows northward to feed the great Yellow and Yangtze rivers. The moisture and temperate climates of these zones made them early cradles of agricultural civilization.

As the moisture-laden flows move north, they cool and release their moisture. And because the moisture content of these flows is increasing with rising temperatures, intense flooding episodes are becoming more common. If warm, water-heavy pockets of air become stalled over a region, a large share of the moisture can be released in a single location, causing downpours and flooding events that will become more intense as surface temperatures rise. In the summer of 2024, Europe, China, and the eastern United States all experienced such destructive flooding events.

One of the puzzles of climate change is that while it drives more intense downpours and flooding, as warmer airs hold and transport greater moisture, it also has intensified aridity, and associated wildfires and desertification. If warmer air holds more moisture, why are some areas getting drier? The consequences of this trend are especially devastating in the western United States and Canada, where longer dry seasons are turning forests into kindling.

Let's focus on one of those areas facing increasing aridity: California's Central Valley and Inland Empire. This area is one of the most productive agricultural regions of the United States, and it is increasingly threatened by climate change. A combination of heat and aridity are threatening crops and creating an alarming formula for forest fires. To understand why it is getting more arid, we need to follow the winds.

As we saw earlier, winds in the northern temperate zone blow from the west. In California, moisture-laden air blows in off the Pacific. But California has a coastal mountain range, and when those winds run into the mountains, they are forced up and over the top. As the air rises, air pressure falls, and the temperature drops—this decrease in temperature due to decreasing pressure is called adiabatic cooling. At a higher altitude, the cool air holds less moisture and releases its excess moisture as rain or dew. The windward side of California's coastal range is lush from abundant rainfall.

As the wind drops down the eastern side of the coastal range, it warms again and regains its ability to hold moisture. This warm-but-dry wind is like a wrung-out sponge, ready to soak up any water in its path. As it crosses California's Central Valley, it evaporates rivers, lakes, and water held in the soil, causing them to dry up. We see similar effects in South America, where Chile's Atacama Desert, tucked in behind the Andean Range, is among the driest ecologies on Earth. We also see it in Europe, where the coastal range on the Iberian Peninsula leaves the land to its east arid and prone to fires. India's Deccan Plateau, sheltered behind the large coastal Ghats ranges, is also getting drier.

For many of these regions, the impact of evaporative drying of the land is seasonal, occurring primarily in the warm, dry months. Historically, rain that accumulated as mountain snowpack during the winters provided a steady supply of meltwater during the summer, and humans built an elaborate irrigation infrastructure to channel it toward arid farmlands through the summer. But the streams and dams that funnel and store that water are everywhere losing their vitality.

The problem is primarily one of storage. With higher temperatures, less of the wet-season precipitation is being stored in high-mountain snowpack. From the Sierras and Rockies in the United States to the Pyrenees and Alps in Europe and the Himalayas in South Asia, glaciers and snow volume are decreasing. The massive mountain-fed rivers that have historically helped to sustain agricultural irrigation through the summer in these areas are losing volume. Arid agricultural regions that rely on summer irrigation fed by streams of mountain meltwater are coming under increasing threat. If they are to sustain their farming futures, engineers will have to build new capacity to store water that can be tapped for use during the long, dry summer months. This means more dams and reservoirs, as well as projects to bank water underground by actively replenishing regional water tables.

Modeling these hydrological systems represents one of the most challenging components of the GCMs. But behind that complexity, one rule of thumb remains valid: wet areas are going to get wetter, and dry areas are going to get dryer. In the United States, this means that the Mississippi basin will experience more and stronger rains, while the western United States will continue to lose ground water.

There is one important exception to this generalization: tropical forests. In regions like the Amazon rainforest or the vast jungles of Indonesia, roughly half of the moisture in the air comes from transpiration, the evaporation from the leaves of vegetation in the jungle itself. As plants absorb life-giving carbon dioxide to power their chlorophyl, they also give off oxygen and water to the air. These tropical jungle systems rely on having enough plants and trees to replenish the moisture in the air through evaporation from leaves. As land in these regions is being cleared for agriculture, the jungles are feeding less moisture into the air. At some point in the future, we may reach a tipping point at which the air over these jungles begins to dry out. When that happens, the vast stores of carbon held in the tropical rainforests will be released as these lands transform into semi-arid savanna landscapes.

Rising Tides, Stronger Storms

One of the most dramatic impacts of climate change has been the rise in sea levels. On the timescale at which we live our lives, the progression appears slow. Today, higher global temperatures are causing oceans to rise at roughly 4 millimeters per year, or 4 centimeters (1.5 inches) per decade. But these are only averages. What matters for coastal habitation are the extremes associated with high tides and storm surges—when strong surface winds drive waters toward shore. These lead to flooding and often the infiltration of salt water into freshwater sources on land and below ground. Depending on how rapidly we act to hold back climate change, sea levels are projected to rise between one and eight feet by the end of the century.

Rising tides have two causes. About half of the sea-level rise we have experienced to date has been caused by melting glaciers and ice sheets. As water held as ice in mountain glaciers and in the Antarctic and Greenland ice sheets melts, that runoff raises the global sea level. Scientists have estimated that the water stored as ice on Greenland and Antarctica alone could, if it melted entirely, raise the global sea level by over 250 feet. The major source of ice loss in both places occurs via glaciers. These slow-moving rivers of ice carry vast volumes of frozen water from inland to the coast where they break off, or calve, as icebergs. The speed of flow of glaciers is a critical driver of sea-level rise, and there are signs that some of the largest glaciers in Greenland and Antarctica are accelerating. The Jakobshavn Glacier on the west coast of Greenland and the Thwaites Glacier in West Antarctica are the focus of particular scientific attention.

The other cause of sea-level rise is thermal expansion. As water warms, it expands. This is true of most liquids: additional energy (heat) causes the molecules to oscillate more energetically, and the molecular structure spreads out. The effect is relatively small. At the scale of a glass of water, for example, the thermal expansion caused by raising the temperature would be impossible to detect with the human eye. At the scale of the ocean, however, the effect is significant. Earth's average sea surface temperature has risen by about 1.5°C (3°F) since 1900. Most of the warming has been limited to the upper hundred or so meters of the ocean. With this much water involved, the thermal expansion of water has a significant effect. A 100-meter column of water that is warmed by 1.5°C, for example, will expand nearly 7 centimeters (2.8 inches). That accounts for over a third of the total eight inches of sea-level rise we have observed since 1900.

The most visible and destructive consequences of rising ocean temperatures is the role they play in intensifying hurricanes. Hurricanes form when warm ocean water heats the surface air, causing it to rise. That rising air forms a powerful updraft that creates a vacuum at its base. New air is sucked into that vacuum from all directions. Following the dictates of the Coriolis effect, air flowing south into the hurricane center veers to the right. Air flowing north into the center does the same. This creates an accelerating counterclockwise vortex (in the Northern Hemisphere) that is powered by the heat of the ocean. As the ocean temperature is turned up, the intensity of the storm grows. Researchers estimate that a 1°C (1.8°F) increase in water temperature increases hurricane wind speeds by thirty to forty miles per hour.

Concluding Thoughts

Our knowledge of climate change runs the gamut from high confidence to low confidence, depending on which part of the phenomenon we are addressing. It is useful to have in mind which elements we can feel confident about, and which reflect significant uncertainty. In the three-tiered world of climate modeling, the EBMs and GCMs are extremely robust. Some important puzzles remain—about cloud formation, glacier flow, and the fate of the AMOC—and scientists are researching these gaps and making steady progress. But all research groups developing these models agree on the finding that the climate change we are already experiencing is entirely caused by GHG emissions driven by human activity.

The third tier of modeling, focused on the human dimension of climate change, is still largely speculative. The IAMs we use to project how human society will interact with climate change provide useful tools to evaluate policy alternatives, but they are highly diverse in their findings and should be interpreted as suggestive rather than conclusive. The primary source of uncertainty in these models derives from attempts to predict how human society is likely to respond to a changing climate, today and in the future.

One element of the human response to climate change remains particularly under-analyzed and, hence, an area of significant uncertainty. That has to do with the myriad ways in which humans will adapt to a changing climate. Under climate pressure, we will relocate, reinvest, and retrain. It is possible that we will have to rethink how we grow food, how we manufacture products, and how we live and work. We know less about these dimensions of adaptation, in part because climate researchers are hesitant to place adaptation at the forefront of our climate agenda. Rightly or wrongly, they worry about a phenomenon referred to as moral hazard: the risk that a focus on adaptation will reduce our urgency in tackling the root causes of climate change. Ultimately, we will adapt, and as we do so, we will learn more about it. For now, though, one of the most pressing climate challenges for many companies, adaptation, remains understudied.

What adaptation will mean for different sectors and companies necessarily varies widely. Agriculture has already been deeply affected by new patterns of rain and aridity, accompanied by altered pest pressure and new potential regions opening to cultivation. Construction firms increasingly face the impacts of high daytime temperatures on outdoor workers. Transportation and logistics firms must accommodate more frequent and intense disruptions. For some of these problems, companies can rely on insurance for crops, property, or business interruption to manage unexpected disruptions. But because these shocks are part of enduring and widespread trends, insurance provides only a short-term response. Ultimately, companies will have to make significant investments that alter their practices in ways that adapt to our changing climate. Firms that do so in a timely and thoughtful way are likely to reap advantages relative to their competitors.

CHAPTER 4

THE MARKET
FOR CARBON

The atomic element carbon lies at the heart of climate change and our strategy for addressing it. This atom, with six protons, neutrons, and electrons, makes up the core of the two gases that are the main contributors to climate change: carbon dioxide (CO_2), and methane (CH_4). Other gases also contribute to climate change, including sulfur compounds and more complex aromatic hydrocarbons, but the bulk of the warming, 90 percent, is attributable to anthropogenic (human-caused) emissions of CO_2 and CH_4.

This chapter introduces the basic tools we use for measuring the sources and impact of CO_2 and CH_4 emissions. It explains the economic logic of carbon pricing as a tool to reduce emissions, and how appropriate carbon prices can be calculated. Setting an appropriate cost of carbon requires that we measure the cost of climate change, taking into account an appropriate discount rate for valuing future damage. We also consider the idea of the global carbon budget, which describes the amount of additional carbon that can be emitted before we reach the Paris Agreement target of 1.5°C temperature rise. These are the economic tools that policy makers have in mind when they design and assess policy responses to climate change. Each of these topics is discussed in the following sections. We begin, however, with the biosphere's carbon cycle.

Sources of Carbon Emissions

The amount of CO_2 in the air is regulated by the carbon cycle. Bacteria and animals give off CO_2 as a by-product when they use oxygen to break down organic molecules created by plants. Plants in turn absorb CO_2 to fuel photosynthesis. In equilibrium, these flows tend to balance out. Higher levels of oxygen encourage a more rapid increase in the number of animals; higher levels of CO_2 encourage greater plant growth. This balancing effect has helped to buffer the impact of excess human-created carbon emissions. As we emit more CO_2, plants grow faster and larger, allowing them to absorb some of the excess gas that we emit. But the ability of plants to absorb our excess CO_2 emissions is woefully inadequate, a gap that is exasperated by deforestation.

About 650 million years ago, the carbon cycle balance between animals and plants broke down. As plants for the first time found their way onto dry land, animals remained in the oceans. Without animals and bacteria to consume the newly abundant plant and tree mass, their carbon compounds—including cellulose (wood) and lignin (bark)—remained undigested and ultimately were buried in the ground. This was the Carboniferous Age, when oxygen emitted by plants built up in the atmosphere to over twice the concentration we experience today. Over the subsequent hundreds of millions of years, the layers of excess carbon were compressed and converted

THE MARKET FOR CARBON

into what we know today as coal. Nearly all of the coal we have mined and burned during the industrial revolution comes from this period, from 650 million to 600 million years ago.

Oil and gas have a different origin. They mostly are the result of a slow accumulation of blue-green algae that sank to the bottom of the world's oceans and built up there over time. Like coal, these deposits were gradually broken down into carbon-hydrogen molecules (hydrocarbons) of various lengths. Volatile gases like ethane (C_2H_6) and butane (C_4H_{10}) have short carbon chains. Paraffins and asphalt have longer carbon chains and are solid at room temperature. Petroleum we pump from the ground is a mixture of all different sizes and shapes of hydrocarbon molecules (see chapter 5).

By burning fossil fuels, we are extraordinarily rapidly returning carbon compounds to the atmosphere that were removed gradually over millions of years. It is as if we had taken a teaspoon of water out of the tub each time we took a bath, then years later, dumped all of the accumulated water back into the tub.

Deposits of coal, oil, and gas are not the only stores of carbon on Earth. Vegetation and trees hold enormous stocks of carbon as well. The greatest plant stores of carbon are held in the boreal forests of northern North America and Asia, and in the tropical rainforests of the Amazon basin and of Southeast Asia. Burning or clearing of these jungle forests releases a large volume of carbon dioxide into the atmosphere. A large stock of sequestered carbon is also held in plant matter locked into the frozen tundra of the Arctic. As the permafrost of the Arctic melts, bacteria that consume the organic matter contained in the ice are releasing CO_2 and CH_4 into the atmosphere. The Earth's vegetation and permafrost hold roughly ten times the total carbon that humans have emitted so far by burning coal, oil, and gas over the course of the industrial revolution.

CO_2 accounts for roughly two-thirds of all greenhouse gases emitted by human activity. The other third is caused by a combination

66 A CONCISE BUSINESS GUIDE TO CLIMATE CHANGE

of CH_4, nitrous oxide (N_2O), ozone (O_3), and a class of man-made compounds called halogenated hydrocarbons. CH_4 is by far the largest contributor to the greenhouse effect after carbon dioxide, accounting for 25 percent of total warming. Most of the CH_4 emissions caused by humans come from modern agriculture, including from bacterial breakdown of animal and crop waste and from enteric emissions (burps and farts). In many cases, companies are moving to limit these emissions. For example, cows alone account for a quarter of all man-made (anthropogenic) CH_4 emissions. Producers like Nestlé and Starbucks that are major dairy distributors are aware of the outsize role their products play in climate change, and both are engaged in research to develop and build consumer support for non-dairy alternatives. Oil and gas extraction also emits significant CH_4. Since these emissions can provide a free source of natural gas, energy companies are increasingly working to capture them. Anaerobic bacteria that digest waste in human landfills are another important source of CH_4 emissions. Restaurants and grocery stores are increasingly finding that limiting food waste helps reduce CH_4 emissions while lowering their operating costs.

For accounting purposes, we group all of the greenhouse gases together in order to capture their total impact on climate. To do this, the impact of each gas is expressed in terms of its warming effect relative to CO_2. How much each gas contributes to global warming depends both on how much infrared radiation it absorbs, and on how long the gas remains in the atmosphere. CH_4, for example, is a powerful greenhouse gas, but its molecules are broken down relatively quickly by ultraviolet light from the sun. The average period over which they break down is just twelve years. CO_2 is a less powerful greenhouse gas, but it is more durable; it remains in the atmosphere for an estimated 120 years. To make an apples-to-apples comparison of the warming effect of CH_4 to CO_2, we use a measure that combines intensity and duration, called the global warming

TABLE 4-1

Global warming potential

Greenhouse gas (GHG)	Atmospheric lifetime (years)	Global warming potential (GWP)
Carbon dioxide (CO_2)	50 to 200	1
Methane (CH_4)	12±3	28
Nitrous oxide (N_2O)	120	310
Hydrofluorocarbons (HFCs)	1.5 to 209	150 to 11,700

Source: Intergovernmental Panel on Climate Change, *Climate Change 2021: The Physical Science Basis. Contribution of Working Group I to the Sixth Assessment Report of the Intergovernmental Panel on Climate Change* (Cambridge, UK: Cambridge University Press, 2023), https://www.ipcc.ch/report/ar6/wg1/downloads/report/IPCC_AR6_WGI_FullReport.pdf.

potential (GWP). The GWP for CO_2 is set by definition at 1. The larger the GWP, the more a gas warms the atmosphere for a fixed amount that is emitted. The GWP for CH_4, for example, is 28, making it a powerful greenhouse gas. If we multiply the quantity of each gas emitted by its GWP and add them together, we get total greenhouse gas emissions measured as CO_2 equivalent (CO_2e). (See table 4-1.)

The Social Cost of Carbon

Economists approach climate using tools developed at the beginning of the twentieth century to think about the environmental impact of industrialization. At that time, policy makers tried to understand how they should respond to the societal impact of factory smoke and river pollution. These pollutants were a by-product of industry, and they hurt people who were not directly involved in running the factory. The reality that private businesses were imposing costs on third parties created a challenge for Adam Smith's idea that individual self-interest would also increase the public welfare.

Economists at the time referred to these third-party impacts as externalities, and they posed a special problem for regulators. While pollution from burning coal caused damage, stopping pollution risked limiting the benefits that came from products and jobs that the factory produced. How were policy makers to find the right balance between the interests of the factory owners and workers, and the costs to third parties?

In 1920, a British economist named Arthur Pigou published a six-hundred-page tome entitled *The Economics of Welfare*, in which he proposed an answer to this puzzle—an answer that remains the primary way we think about pollution and climate change today. Pigou's idea was that society should add up the costs of environmental externalities—the cost of river pollution to downstream beer brewers, for example, and of having to burn lamps longer due to darkened skies from coal smoke—and then tax the factory at a rate that exactly matched those costs. Pigou's idea was that companies forced to pay the cost of externalities would in turn make optimal decisions about how, and how much, to emit. We call this approach a Pigouvian tax, and it is the main strategy economists advocate for in addressing the societal costs of climate change today. By taxing CO_2 emissions, governments force companies to take into account the broader societal costs of their emissions.

But how much should emitting companies be taxed? This turns out to be a complicated question, in part because future generations will certainly bear the heaviest costs from climate change. Most of the CO_2 emitted today will remain in the atmosphere for over a century. In principle, emitters should be taxed at a rate that captures the damage caused by those emissions over that entire time. The lifetime damage caused by current carbon emissions we call the social cost of carbon.

While the idea of the social cost of carbon is simple, any actual measurement must face three challenges. First, we have to measure emissions. For many sectors, this is a matter of measuring how much fossil fuels are consumed, since burning fossil fuels produces a predictable amount of CO_2. Other sources of emissions are far harder to tabulate. Forestry and agricultural emissions, for example, are especially challenging to measure, and CH_4 emission remains an area of significant uncertainty.

Second, we have to rely on our integrated assessment models (IAMs) to evaluate the likely economic impact of those emissions over time. The costs are highly varied in kind. Some costs will take the form of reinforcing seawalls and relocating farmland. Other costs are health related, such as rising rates of infectious disease or heat-related injuries. Still further costs relate to companies' lost revenue. Moreover, because there is little consensus about how to design IAMs, policy makers commonly rely on several at once, generating high variance in future cost estimates.

Once we have estimated these future costs, there remains a third problem that has proved especially vexing to advocates of a Pigouvian response to climate change. In conventional financial accounting, we undervalue, or discount, future costs and benefits. The degree to which we undercount them is called the discount rate. Estimating a discount rate for future climate damage has proved especially contentious.

The Discounting Debate

The idea of the discount rate comes out of corporate accounting, where companies use it to calculate the current value of future income and expenditures. The idea is linked to the return on investments. Since any income received today can be invested and generate a return, we should value it more than future income that will have less time to be invested. Because returns on investment define the

70   A CONCISE BUSINESS GUIDE TO CLIMATE CHANGE

difference between current and future earnings, firms typically choose the average cost of capital, expressed as an interest rate, as their discount rate. While the exact number will depend on the details of corporate finance, a typical corporate discount rate is 10 percent.

When economists apply this discounting idea to calculate the social cost of carbon, they discount future climate-related damage at a rate that approximates the average return on investments in the economy. Typical carbon pricing models set the climate discount rate at between 2 percent and 7 percent. One of the most prominent advocates for a carbon tax, the Nobel Prize–winning economist William Nordhaus, favors a climate discount rate of 4.3 percent. Another prominent estimate, produced by the British economist Nicholas Stern, placed the discount rate at 1.4 percent. Whichever rate they choose, by estimating likely future costs of greenhouse gas emissions and discounting them to reflect a present cost, economists can propose a carbon tax rate that will exactly equal the social cost of the climate externality.[1]

A particular challenge to this discounting approach is that the greatest costs of climate change lie far in the future. Yet, in a world of discounting, the further in the future costs occur, the less weight we afford them as we translate them into the social cost of carbon today. This implies that an optimal carbon tax rate will rise over time, reflecting higher costs as we move into a future in which the economic and social toll of climate change is growing greater. Using the 4.3 percent discount rate and an average climate impact projection, Nordhaus prescribes a carbon tax that rises from roughly $40 per ton of emitted CO_2 in the 2020s, to $70 per ton emitted in 2100.[2]

A critical point about this carbon pricing exercise is that it is intended to reduce carbon emissions at a rate that is economically efficient. That means that any other rate of mitigation—either slower or faster—would cost us more as a society. But it turns out that an optimal adjustment path is likely to imply relatively high final temperature increases. Under Nordhaus's scenario, global temperatures would increase by an estimated 3.5°C by 2100—well above the 1.5°C commitment that would later be set in the Paris Agreement. Not surprisingly, the relatively high discount rate Nordhaus uses has been criticized for ignoring the long-term, systemic impacts that a 3.5°C temperature increase is likely to imply.[3] See the sidebar "The Carbon Pricing Debate" for more about this issue.

In reality, few countries have relied on such calculations in order to design a carbon tax that reflects the social cost of carbon. Of countries that use carbon taxes to reduce greenhouse gas emissions, tax rates vary from $24 per ton of emitted carbon dioxide in Ireland to $136 per ton in Sweden. These different tax rates typically reflect the complex politics of imposing carbon taxes rather than an optimal economic calculation.

Even if they are rarely incorporated into the design of carbon taxes, discount rates and calculations of the social cost of carbon matter deeply for how environmental regulations are designed. In the United States, federal regulators have since the early 1980s been required to conduct a cost-benefit analysis for any new regulation. For example, cost-benefit calculations are used to set Corporate Average Fuel Economy (CAFE) standards for US automobile manufacturers. Similar calculations guide the US Army Corps of Engineers (USACE) in its decisions about where to construct the levees and embankments that will help us to adapt to rising seas and stronger storms. Currently, the calculated societal benefit of a USACE project that reduces the impact of climate change must be at least 3.5 times greater than the project's cost. These regulatory applications also highlight the stakes involved in choosing an appropriate discount rate. A high discount rate, for example, will

The Carbon Pricing Debate

Responses to climate change that rely on an economically efficient carbon price—one that exactly internalizes the climate externalities of burning fossil fuels—have been the focus of considerable criticism. Some argue that this approach is being used to justify a slow response that will result in significantly higher future temperatures. Even moderate climate forecasts generate warming projections well above 1.5°C if we focus on optimizing social welfare by using Pigouvian carbon taxes. Others worry that we are undervaluing low probability-but-catastrophic climate scenarios. Rapid permafrost melting or aridification of the Amazon basin could create tipping-point events that would lead to catastrophic outcomes. Because such events are unlikely, they don't have much impact on estimates of average future costs of climate change. Yet, as the global Covid-19 pandemic reminded us, the costs of even unlikely events can be extraordinarily high. It might make sense to pay more, in the form of a more aggressive program of decarbonization, as a form of insurance against such highly undesirable outcomes.

A third set of critics focus on the way the social cost of carbon is calculated. They argue that it is unethical to discount the damage climate change will do to future generations. Why, they ask, should our lives be valued more than theirs? At the very least, these critics push for a lower discount rate, typically of 1 or 2 percent. This has the effect of raising the social cost of carbon significantly, thereby speeding our response to climate change. Some countries have been responsive to this criticism. The United Kingdom has since 2003 reduced the discount rate for longer-term costs. For the first thirty years, climate costs are discounted at 3.5 percent; for climate costs incurred between thirty and a hundred years, the discount rate is lowered to 1.5 percent; beyond a hundred years, it is set at 1 percent. This kind of declining discount rate is justified in part by the growing uncertainty around longer-term cost projections.

reduce the weight placed on potential long-term benefits of these policies.

As climate costs are mostly in the future, regulatory cost-benefit analyses also need to employ a discount rate. In the United States, that rate is set by executive order, which means it also changes from administration to administration. The Obama and Biden administrations, for example, adopted a 3 percent discount rate; the first Trump administration adopted a 7 percent discount rate. Because the choice to use a lower discount rate amplifies the future cost of climate change, it increases the benefits of more aggressive climate action today. By contrast, a higher discount rate reduces the current cost of future climate damage. Just moving from a 3 percent discount rate to a 7 percent discount rate can decrease the social cost of carbon by a factor of ten. Using their different discount rates, the Trump administration estimated the social cost of carbon at about $5, while the Biden administration estimated the price at $50.

A Carbon Budget

Both business and environmental activists have expressed support for carbon taxes as a response to climate change. Yet policy makers have not primarily relied on carbon taxes in their response to climate change. More common has been an alternative approach that directly regulates the volume of CO_2 emissions. These emissions restrictions are typically applied via a system of tradable permits, such that any company can buy the right to emit from another company. The European Union Emissions Trading System (EU ETS), the US Regional Greenhouse Gas Initiative (RGGI), and California's cap-and-trade program all rely on tradable permits to limit emissions in the electricity-generation sector. Some regional governments in China have launched CO_2 cap-and-trade schemes, and India is also introducing a nationwide cap-and-trade program.

All cap-and-trade programs operate in a similar way. First, a central authority issues a limited number of emissions permits for a given compliance period. In RGGI, compliance periods span three years. In the EU ETS, the compliance period has progressively expanded from five to eight to ten years. Second, allocated permits are put into circulation either by distribution to historical emitters, or through an auction process. Third, companies must hand in permits to cover their total emissions at the end of each compliance period. Companies that are not able to reduce their emissions enough to meet the number of permits they own may purchase permits from other companies. Companies with excess permits may in turn sell them or bank them for the subsequent compliance period. To ensure emissions reduction, the number of allocated permits is reduced over time. The prospect of lower future quantity and rising prices for carbon credits has led some investors to buy and bank permits that they intend to sell in a later compliance period.

Cap-and-trade regimes have been praised for their economic efficiency and direct impact on CO_2 emissions. Because permits to emit may be traded, companies with the lowest cost of reduction undertake emissions reductions. This leads to the lowest-possible cost for reducing emissions. In fact, economically, the cap-and-trade and carbon tax approaches are both efficient and really two sides of the same coin: one raises the price of carbon in order to lower emissions; the other reduces allowable emissions and thereby raises the price of carbon. Confusingly, many writers refer to both schemes as a carbon tax.

Yet the two approaches have important differences, and some features of the cap-and-trade approach have made it more politically popular. First, the climate impact of cap-and-trade is direct. Policy makers set the volume of emissions they wish to allow,

THE MARKET FOR CARBON

and companies meet that target. This allows policy makers to set a global carbon budget and then determine how that budget should be allocated across countries and over time. To meet the 1.5°C target for the global average temperature increase set in the Paris Agreement, for example, researchers estimate that we as a global society can only emit roughly 400 gigatons of additional carbon. Given that our annual global emissions were roughly 36 gigatons in 2023, and rising, it suggests we could only emit at current levels for another decade and still come in under our agreed-on temperature target. A realistic chance at meeting the 1.5°C target will require that we tighten our carbon budget dramatically in the near term so that it can be extended to the full three decades that the green transition is expected to require.

The second attraction of cap-and-trade relates to the way in which permits are distributed. In Europe, roughly half of carbon emission permits are required to be allocated for free to companies that have historically had high emissions. These free allocations will sunset in 2027. The other half are sold at auction, and that auctioned share is increasing over time. The free allocations are designed to discourage high emitters in Europe from fleeing to other countries without a similar cap-and-trade scheme. This kind of climate migration is referred to as leakage. Directly distributed permits are also politically attractive, as they serve to compensate politically powerful historical emitters that face high future transition costs. European coal generators, for example, will be hurt by the move to renewable energy; free allocations under the EU ETS gives them a financial lifeline.

Cap-and-trade schemes do come with costs. Creating functioning markets for credits can be complex. And markets, being what they are, can be volatile. Because cap-and-trade regimes do not set the price of carbon emissions directly—only indirectly by fixing the volume—swings in demand can cause large price shifts. Such price

76   A CONCISE BUSINESS GUIDE TO CLIMATE CHANGE

shifts may be exacerbated by buyers who purchase and bank emissions credits for future commitment periods. The price of carbon permits within the EU ETS, for example, jumped from €5 to €30 in 2018, almost entirely due to investors betting on higher future prices. To reduce the impact of such price volatility on emitting companies, both the EU ETS and RGGI have created market reserve funds that buy and sell carbon credits in order to place upper and lower bounds on carbon prices.

Carbon Offsets

One attractive feature of cap-and-trade regimes is that they are easy to integrate with markets for carbon offsets. Carbon offsets represent greenhouse gases that are removed from the air and sequestered. They may also be accredited to projects that stop the emission of greenhouse gases that would otherwise have occurred. Carbon offsets are measured in dollars per ton of carbon ($/ton C)—the same units as cap-and-trade permits—and many cap-and-trade regimes allow the use of carbon offsets to qualify for some share of a firm's greenhouse gas emissions.[4]

The point at which human-caused greenhouse gas emissions are entirely offset by carbon sequestration activities is referred to as net zero. Because it implies no further human impact on atmospheric carbon content, this net-zero point has become the focus for national, global, and corporate climate planning. The Intergovernmental Panel on Climate Change's *Sixth Assessment Report*, published in 2021, foresees a pathway to net zero by roughly 2060 that combines an 80 percent reduction in greenhouse gas emissions from current levels with 20 percent carbon sequestration primarily in soil and the oceans. For companies that have set a net-zero target, the purchase of carbon offsets generated by greenhouse gas sequestration projects is also typically an important tool in their overall climate strategy.

Carbon offsets that are used to meet statutory emissions-reduction requirements under regional cap-and-trade regimes must be certified by an accrediting agency. California's cap-and-trade program, for example, relies on the nongovernmental agency Verra to certify carbon offsets. The kinds of offsets that can be counted toward emissions are defined by law. California currently recognizes five categories of projects as qualifying for offsets:

- Afforestation and reforestation

- Dairy enteric methane reduction

- Mine methane capture

- Soil capture in rice cultivation

- Projects mitigating ozone-depleting substances

Whatever the project type, all verified offsets must meet two criteria. The first is additionality. Any project certified for carbon offset credits must reduce carbon emissions *beyond* what would have occurred in the absence of the program. Cutting down a forest to plant another would not typically meet the additionality requirement. The second criterion is permanence. Any project certified for carbon offset credits has to reduce atmospheric carbon in a durable way. If a planted forest subsequently burns, it does not meet the durability standard. The typical duration required to meet the durability standard is one hundred years.

Carbon offsets that are verified by certified third-party organizations like Verra are called compliance-grade offsets. They represent the gold-standard of carbon offsetting. While they are primarily used to meet statutory emissions targets in regions with cap-and-trade systems, like Europe and California, they are also increasingly

78   A CONCISE BUSINESS GUIDE TO CLIMATE CHANGE

being purchased by companies that are opting to set voluntary carbon net-zero targets. Compliance-grade offsets may be purchased either on carbon offset exchanges, such as the London-based Carbon TradeXchange, or through direct contracting between off-takers and carbon sequestration project operators.

Offsets and Their Critics

Although they play an important role in our long-term strategy for redressing greenhouse gas emissions, carbon offsets have also been the subject of considerable criticism. Partly in response to these criticisms, most cap-and-trade schemes that accept carbon offsets also limit how many can be counted toward the emissions cap. California's cap-and-trade program, for example, limits carbon offsets to 4 percent of the total emissions budget. Corporations are also increasingly committing to limit their use of carbon offsets to meet their internal emissions targets. One of the most widely used corporate decarbonization protocols, promulgated by the nonprofit Science Based Targets initiative (SBTi), currently recommends limiting corporate use of carbon offsets to 10 percent of total reductions. While in principle the buying and selling of emissions offsets still represents the most efficient way to reduce global emissions, a number of practical and ethical concerns have made companies increasingly wary of this strategy.

The controversy around offsets has three main sources. First, critics worry that some approved carbon offsets may not meet the additionality and permanence standards. Europe offers a cautionary tale. As originally conceived, Europe's EU ETS accepted carbon offsets called certified emissions reductions (CERs) that were created under the 1997 UN Kyoto Protocol for meeting domestic emissions targets. CERs in the UN system were generated by projects undertaken in poor countries under the provisions of the Clean Development Mechanism and certified by a global network of approved standards agencies. Early renewable energy projects in China and India generated CERs, for example, which they sold to European companies, generating additional revenue streams. But Europe increasingly worried that the standards agencies were being too lax, and in the wake of a series of offset scandals involving judgments about additionality, stopped accepting CERs to meet EU ETS limits. Europe's new carbon trading scheme for civil aviation is planning to reintroduce carbon offsets, but under European certifying authority.

A related certification concern comes from a risk of double counting. If a corporation purchases an offset from a foreign country, for example, and that offset is also used to achieve the emissions target of that country, the sequestered or reduced carbon emission is being counted twice. Careful accounting and tracking are required to ensure that one offset activity is not double counted in this way.

A second potential concern about the use of carbon offsets is the duration of time for which carbon removed from the atmosphere must be sequestered. Some technologies for sequestering carbon might potentially be only temporary, depending on accidents or future decisions. Research shows that carbon sequestered in the soil through no-till farming, for example, may be quickly re-emitted if farming practices change. Carbon sequestered in new forests is re-emitted in case of forest fires.

The IPCC sets a standard of at least one-hundred-year guaranteed sequestration in order to meet the standard of permanence. This standard has been adopted by the major certification bodies. Verra, for example, allows offset providers to achieve permanence in different ways. Forestry projects are required to set aside 10 percent to 15 percent of the carbon offsets they generate as a buffer. These offsets are canceled in the case of a forest fire that destroys trees that were used to create offsets.[5] Certifying bodies also favor forestry

80   A CONCISE BUSINESS GUIDE TO CLIMATE CHANGE

that supports wood for use in construction, since this wood is less likely to be burned and release its sequestered carbon into the atmosphere. Forests grown for firewood or pulping are not typically eligible for certified offset credits. The number of current offset projects that don't meet the permanence principle is potentially quite large.

Other strategies for generating carbon offsets include new technologies that combine different technologies for carbon capture and storage. Carbon may be captured at the point of emission, as with the use of CO_2 scrubbers on the emissions of coal plants, or with new direct air capture technologies that pull carbon out of the air or water. Both technologies remain expensive. Once captured, carbon may be reused in industrial applications or stored in a variety of ways. These include underground storage, in which CO_2 is injected into space left by the extraction of natural gas, or as stable solid materials such as biochar or converted to minerals. The general strategy of capturing and then storing carbon is called carbon capture and storage (CCS), and researchers are experimenting with a vast range of technologies to do so in a cost-effective way. Given the large, expected reliance on carbon sequestration, the future market for CCS services is potentially vast.

A final criticism of carbon offsets focuses on the way they distribute the burden of carbon emissions reduction. Carbon sequestration projects tend to be less expensive in poorer countries, giving them a price advantage in the carbon offset market. Corporations in affluent countries that meet their net-zero targets by purchasing carbon offsets from poor countries risk being criticized for asking poor countries to solve a problem that they had little role in creating. This is one way in which questions of climate justice affect how markets for emissions reduction are designed and implemented.

Over time, standards and practices around the definition and ethical implications of carbon offsets should become clearer and more robust. Whether we ultimately end up with a single global carbon price, or a range of carbon offset products of different quality and price, is an open question. For now, the international framework for carbon offset markets, defined under Article 6.4 of the Paris Agreement, remains a work in progress. In the absence of adequate formal standards, a new group of carbon-credit-rating platforms has emerged to evaluate and rate different carbon offset products. Given this level of uncertainty, firms are increasingly relying on carbon reductions along their supply chains, in the form of carbon insets, to help reduce emissions in a cost-effective way.

Concluding Thoughts

There is perhaps no part of the climate change response where theory and practice are more at odds than in the realm of carbon markets and pricing. On the one hand, our economic theories of carbon taxes and efficient emissions reduction are well developed. For economists and policy makers who have been engaged in this work, the solution to climate change amounts to the implementation of a properly-scaled carbon tax. On the other hand, national regulation and practice around carbon markets and pricing is highly fragmented and, in some cases, beset by fraud. There would seem to be little hope that theory and practice will soon meet.

For firms navigating the turbulent waters of decarbonization, carbon markets present both an opportunity and a risk. While purchasing carbon offsets can in principle offer the most cost-effective means for many firms to pursue decarbonization, customers and investors may be less impressed with this approach than economists tend to be. Moreover, norms and standards of accounting for emissions and certifying offsets are still emerging and evolving. For the moment, patience and caution remain the most important principles.

CHAPTER 5

GREEN ENERGY TRANSITION

This chapter focuses on the economics and politics of transitioning from fossil fuels to renewable energy sources. It introduces the economics of energy, including pricing, fixed and variable costs, base and peak load, and transmission and storage. It also discusses the renewables technologies that are likely to replace fossil fuels, including wind, solar, geothermal, nuclear, batteries, green hydrogen, and green ammonia. It then traces the likely transition trajectory, and the economic and political implications of the renewables-based economy.

About three-quarters of greenhouse gases we emit into the atmosphere come from burning fossil fuels. Of those, a quarter come from electricity generation, and the rest from heating buildings, powering transportation, and powering industry. As buildings, transportation, and industry seek to decarbonize, demands for electricity generation and transmission will increase substantially. That means new renewables will not only have to replace existing fossil fuel capacity in electricity generation, but also likely increase our future capacity substantially. In the United States, electricity consumption is projected to double by 2050. As this happens, the electrical grid capacity will also have to double.

While we are still at the beginning of the transition away from fossil fuels, much of how that transition will occur is already becoming clear. Whatever strategies and technologies we ultimately rely on to decarbonize our economies, the shift to renewable energy sources will transform many aspects of our society. In this chapter, we look at the relative merits of fossil fuels and renewables, their economic and technical features, and their climate impact.

Power, Energy, and CO_2

First, let's introduce how we measure electricity. When we discuss electricity generation and consumption, we use two different measurements. One captures the rate of energy generation and use; the other, the quantity of energy supplied and used.

The rate at which energy is produced and flows into the electric grid at any moment is called power and is measured in megawatts (millions of watts, or MW) or gigawatts (billions of watts, or GW). Power plants, for example, are typically described in terms of the maximum gigawatts of power they can provide to the electrical grid. A typical coal plant might have 1 GW capacity. Modern offshore wind turbines have power capacities ranging from 5 to 10 MW. The Hornsea 2 wind farm off the east coast of England, for example, one of the largest in the world, combines 165 8 MW wind turbines to produce 1.3 GW of power.

Megawatts and gigawatts both measure the rate of flow of energy; they don't describe the *quantity* of energy produced or consumed.

How much energy does a factory use each day? How much energy does an electric vehicle (EV) need to travel a hundred miles? To measure these quantities of energy, we calculate the power consumed over the course of an hour, defined as megawatt hours (MWh) or, for smaller applications like EVs or individual houses, kilowatt hours (KWh). A typical EV battery, for example, can hold 50–75 KWh, enough energy to carry it two hundred to three hundred miles. The average American consumes 4.5 MWh of residential electricity per year; the average German consumes 1.7 MWh per year.

The price of electricity is measured either in dollars per MWh ($/MWh) or in cents per KWh (¢/KWh). The price can vary significantly across regions, seasons, and times of the day. In the United States, residential electricity rates range from 6¢/KWh to up to 70¢/KWh, depending on fuel source, transmission costs, and demand conditions. US commercial electricity rates tend to be lower, ranging from 5¢/KWh to 30¢/KWh. For an EV owner in Massachusetts in 2022, for example, fully charging the vehicle from their residential electric supply would cost $10–$15. When comparing fossil fuel energy to renewable energy sources for use in electricity generation, we commonly compare the cost of generation per KWh. We'll look at that comparison later in this chapter, when we look more closely at renewables.

Before we do so, however, we need to know something about how we have traditionally generated electricity. That has focused on three fossil fuels: petroleum, natural gas, and coal.

Petroleum

Petroleum, also called crude oil, is a mixture of large and small hydrocarbons that have a range of uses in our modern economy. The remnants of aquatic microorganisms, petroleum exists in a large number of locations around the world, with the largest known deposits in the Middle East, Central Siberia, the North Sea, the Gulf of Mexico, West Texas, off the east coast of Africa, and in the oil sands of Alberta, Canada.

Not all petroleum that comes out of the ground is created equal. Some has low viscosity and flows easily at room temperature. This is called "light" crude. "Heavy" crude has a larger share of large tar and bitumen compounds and can be extremely viscous or nearly solid at room temperature. Even light crude may not flow well in low temperatures, as in winter. For that reason, oil is kept warm for transport and processing. The Alaska pipeline, which carries crude oil eight hundred miles from Prudhoe Bay on Alaska's North Slope south to Valdez, Alaska, just east of Anchorage, is heated to 140°F along the route. Lighter petroleum has a higher concentration of gasoline and kerosine components and tends to be more highly valued.

The other important difference among sources of petroleum is the amount of sulfur they include. Sulfur compounds are corrosive and have to be removed prior to processing, thereby increasing the cost of oil refining. Petroleum with low sulfur levels is referred to as "sweet." High-sulfur petroleum is called "sour." Petroleum that is both low-viscosity and low in sulfur is called "sweet light" crude and is the most desirable. Both US crude oil from West Texas and Brent crude oil from the North Sea are sweet light crude. Petroleum from the Middle East tends to be heavy and sour, although some oil fields there also produce sweet light crude.

Oil also varies widely in its cost of extraction. Saudi Arabia is among the cheapest producers in the world, with a cost of extraction around $3 per barrel. (Each barrel holds 42 gallons of crude.) Mid-price producing regions, including the Permian Basin in West Texas and Russian onshore fields in Siberia, have extraction costs around $20 per barrel. Regions that require greater investment and technology to extract the oil, including the Alberta tar sands in Canada and offshore production in the United Kingdom, can cost upward of $40 per barrel. New extraction technologies, like horizontal drilling and hydraulic fracturing ("fracking"), are helping to make new oil sources economically viable.

Despite the differing extraction costs, and differences in the qualities of the extracted petroleum, the price for crude oil tends to be very similar globally. Standard benchmark prices are based on specific kinds of oil, such as West Texas Intermediate or Brent crude oil from the North Sea. Crude oil is sold on both spot markets and futures markets. About half of oil sales are purchased through futures contracts, and the prices of those contracts are what we use to report the daily price of oil. Among the most commonly reported global crude oil prices, for example, is the futures price for West Texas Intermediate Light Sweet Crude Oil (WTI). Crude oil consumers such as refineries may contract a price for crude oil up to nine years into the future.

Crude oil is composed of a range of hydrocarbon compounds that have to be separated out through refining. First the sulfur is removed from the oil. It is then put through a continuous distillation process in a device called a fractionating column. This happens in a refinery, where oil is pumped into a vertical column that is heated from the bottom. As the oil warms, smaller molecules that vaporize at low temperatures rise toward the top of the column, where they condense. Large carbon molecules with high boiling points take more heat to vaporize and condense toward the bottom of the column. By separating out the organic compounds in oil by their boiling points, oil refineries are able to extract a wide range of valuable organic compounds.

Some are small, light molecules like methane (CH_4) and ethane (C_2H_6). These are gases at room temperature and are captured from the very top of the fractionating column. Methane is the dominant component of natural gas (90 percent to 95 percent), along with a small amount (5 percent to 10 percent) of ethane. Historically, that gas was burned as it was vented from the column, a practice called

A CONCISE BUSINESS GUIDE TO CLIMATE CHANGE

flaring. Today, most methane and ethane separated from crude oil is captured and used. The methane is sold as natural gas. Recovered ethane goes to produce the polyethylene (PE) plastics that are used in products ranging from plastic bags to medical equipment. A third of all plastics produced on earth are made with PE.

Larger organic molecules separated from crude oil are liquid at room temperature. These include most of the liquid fuels we consume for heating and mobility, including gasoline (petrol), kerosene, and diesel. These liquid fuels make up three-quarters of all crude oil by weight. Still larger molecules, including aromatic (ring-shaped) hydrocarbons, are separated out to make lubricants, tar, asphalt, and paraffin.

Because oil is separated into so many different useful products, each of which requires its own handling and transport, crude oil refineries are typically located closer to consumers of those products than to where the oil is extracted. The global petroleum industry is organized around the principle of shipping crude oil to *where* it is needed and storing it *until* it is needed. This means that oil-rich countries without much domestic demand for fossil fuels often do not have their own refineries. Developing countries that are oil-rich, like Nigeria and Angola, may export petroleum, while also importing kerosene and diesel from a refinery in a third country. This means gas for heating, cooking, and transportation can be especially expensive in developing countries, even those with abundant petroleum resources, and their governments commonly subsidize those fuels. One study has estimated that half of the cost of kerosene used by households in developing countries is paid for by government subsidies.[1]

Natural Gas and Coal

The fastest-growing fossil fuel over the past thirty years has been natural gas. Natural gas is mostly methane, which is a natural by-product of the anaerobic (not involving oxygen) breakdown of organic molecules. Much of the natural gas we burn was formed from the remains of marine microorganisms like blue-green algae that died and accumulated on the seabed and were later covered by sediment. Both coal mines and oil fields also typically contain reserves of natural gas. The majority of the natural gas we use comes from deposits that are either trapped below a nonporous sedimentary rock layer like shale or held in the gaps of porous sandstone.

Natural gas can be compressed to create a liquid (LNG), which can be transported on trains or ships, and then re-gasified for use. In general, however, LNG is more expensive, and most natural gas (80 percent) is transported as gas through pipelines. Because natural gas distribution is mostly limited to fixed transmission equipment, most gas prices are set as long-term sales contracts that may include stipulations covering both the price and quantity of future purchases. Confusingly, gas prices are typically measured in the imperial British thermal unit (Btu), with roughly 3,400 Btus equaling 1 KWh.

In both Europe and the United States, where extensive gas pipeline networks have been built, spot markets for gas also exist. The benchmark US natural gas price is based on futures prices for gas at a large pipeline junction in Erath, Louisiana, called the Henry Hub. Gas futures contracts traded on the New York Mercantile Exchange are based on "Henry Hub prices" for delivery at that junction. Europe's benchmark gas price is based on futures contracts traded at the Title Transfer Facility (TTF) in the Netherlands. Apart from LNG trade, regional gas markets are usually not connected and may experience very different prices. When Russia invaded Ukraine in the spring of 2022, for example, the TTF natural gas price rose to $40 per millions of Btu (mBtu), while the Henry Hub price hovered around $5 per mBtu.

Coal has different origins from natural gas and petroleum, although most coal deposits also contain small amounts of natural gas. (Natural gas has no smell and was a serious threat to early miners, who called it "firedamp" for the way it dimmed their mining lamps.) Most of the coal that has been mined over the past two centuries dates from a specific geologic period, the Carboniferous. Since Britain began exporting coal in the mid-nineteenth century, coal has been shipped around the world. Like oil, its pricing is global, with spot prices that vary depending on the quality of the coal. The highest-quality coal is called anthracite. Anthracite burns clean and hot and has traditionally been used for residential heating. Bituminous coal, the most common type used in industry and energy generation, has lower energy density and burns less hot. Lignite, also called brown coal, has the lowest concentration of carbon and also the lowest energy density. Bituminous coal accounts for three-quarters of global combustion.

Fossil Fuels and Climate Change

All fossil fuels generate carbon dioxide when they combust, or react with oxygen. Coal, petroleum, and natural gas are all formed of hydrogen-carbon (hydrocarbon) molecules with varying proportions of carbon and hydrogen atoms. When they burn, both the hydrogen and the carbon components bond with oxygen, forming water (H_2O) and carbon dioxide (CO_2). The energy released when those new bonds form creates the heat we rely on to generate electricity, fire furnaces, and run internal combustion engines. The CO_2 produced during combustion is the primary driver of the greenhouse effect that causes climate change.

But not all fossil fuels are equal in their impact on the climate. To see why, we need to look more closely at the chemistry of combustion. Natural gas, for example, is mostly methane (CH_4). It has four hydrogen atoms for every carbon atom. When methane bonds break and the carbon and hydrogen atoms bond with oxygen—that is, when they combust—each molecule of methane forms two water molecules and one molecule of carbon dioxide. Chemists describe the reaction like this:

$$CH_4 \rightarrow 2H_2O + CO_2$$

Since all of the newly formed bonds contribute to the heat of combustion, roughly two-thirds of the energy produced in the reaction comes from creating water.

For larger hydrocarbon molecules, however, the ratio of hydrogen to carbon is smaller. Diesel fuel, for example, is formed from much larger molecules: with an average of 12 carbon atoms and 23 hydrogen atoms: $C_{12}H_{23}$. With roughly two times as much hydrogen as carbon, diesel combustion forms H_2O and CO_2 in nearly equal proportion. That means roughly half of the heat generated in combustion comes from forming CO_2.

Coal is by far the worst energy source in terms of climate impact. Composed of a mix of large, ring-shaped hydrocarbons, coal contains hydrogen and carbon atoms in roughly equal proportion. When it combusts, coal forms two CO_2 molecules for every one H_2O molecule. (The products of combustion have to have the same proportion of hydrogen and carbon as the coal from which they are formed.) That means that two-thirds of the energy produced through coal combustion comes from the formation of carbon dioxide, meaning that for every megawatt of electricity generated, coal produces twice as much CO_2 as natural gas, and 50 percent more than diesel. Just by switching from coal to natural gas, an electricity generator could cut its CO_2 emissions in half.

This is what happened in the United States during the first two decades of the 2000s. Between 2005 and 2020, the United States reduced its coal generation by over 50 percent, replacing it mostly with natural gas. That change alone reduced the CO_2 emissions from US electricity generation—which also relies on oil, nuclear, and renewables—by one-third.

Renewable Sources

Fossil fuels bundle three attributes that have made them extraordinarily attractive as sources of energy. Their extraction has a relatively small geographic footprint. They are relatively easy to transport. And they are easy and efficient to store. Renewable energy—solar, wind, hydro—often don't provide the same convenience as fossil fuels. But they do offer important advantages, even beyond their lack of CO_2 emissions. Increasingly, renewables have become among the cheapest sources of electricity. We will consider their cost later in this chapter. First, we need to introduce the main renewable energy sources we use today.

The most widely used renewable energy sources include hydroelectric, solar photovoltaic, and wind turbines. Hydroelectric power still dominates the world's renewable energy mix, accounting for more than half of the total, but little new capacity is being installed today. Hydroelectric power has the advantage of offering stable supply, as well as variable output to meet fluctuations in demand. For example, most hydro plants reduce their electricity output during the night. One disadvantage is its vulnerability to aridity: in regions where rainfall has decreased, dams may be forced to reduce their generation of power.

The fastest-growing renewables today are solar and wind. Nearly all of the grid-scale solar being installed today uses vast arrays of photovoltaic (PV) panels. The price and efficiency of PV panels has been improving dramatically over the past decade. Even with efficiency gains, however, solar energy is space intensive. In 2020, producing 1 MW of power required about three acres of installed PV panels.[2] To match the power of a typical 300 MW gas turbine generator would require a thousand acres, or one-and-a-half square miles. For countries with high population densities and little open land, PV may compete with agricultural output. There are a number of proposed solutions to the problem of agricultural competition. For example, a recent study found that floating panels on existing water reservoirs could meet a third of the world's renewable power needs without using valuable land and would also reduce evaporation.[3] Solar power also has real advantages. Solar installations are nonpolluting, resilient to price and weather shocks, and provide a revenue stream to landowners who may not have had attractive alternative options for their land.

After hydroelectric, wind turbines are the most abundant source of renewable energy today, and their numbers are growing rapidly. As with solar, wind turbine technologies and prices are both improving rapidly. Because larger turbines are more efficient, the size of towers, blades, and generators has also been growing. A typical onshore turbine installed in 2020 had a three-hundred-foot tower, two-hundred-foot blades, and generated 2.5 MW of power. Offshore wind turbines were typically twice as large and produced three times as much power. A new generation of offshore turbines coming to market in the mid-2020s were still larger, with a 12 MW capacity.

Even as solar and wind energy production has been growing, researchers and entrepreneurs are experimenting with a range of alternatives. Startups in the United States, Russia, and China are working to commercialize small modular nuclear reactors that could be built in large quantities and at relatively low cost. Engineering firms are exploring new geothermal options, including deep-crust geothermal that can provide enough heat to run a conventional power-generation plant. In Europe, some energy-intensive industries

94 A CONCISE BUSINESS GUIDE TO CLIMATE CHANGE

are experimenting with biomass reactors that tap the heat from burning organic waste materials to generate electricity. Biomass generation provides a steady, low-cost energy supply with little fluctuation and a local fuel supply.

Peak and Base Load

One of the major challenges facing the energy system is balancing load. Electricity-generating plants cannot put more electricity into the grid than customers are drawing out of it. And if they do not generate enough electricity to meet demand, customers will experience brownouts and blackouts. That means that generation and distribution operators are constantly balancing the load on the system. They do this by modifying both the supply and demand for electricity.

On the supply side, they have to build in extra capacity to meet periods of high demand. Traditionally, they have done so by combining base-load electricity generation from nuclear and coal with peaking capacity, typically provided by gas turbines. The most common and efficient gas turbines are called combined cycle gas turbines (CCGTs), in which excess heat left over after running a gas turbine is used to turn a secondary steam turbine. CCGTs combine efficiency with rapid cycling that allows them to be turned on and off relatively efficiently to meet short-term needs.

On the demand side, electrical utilities often use variable tariffs to encourage or discourage consumption in periods of normally low or high usage. In some cases, as with the Texas power grid supervisor, the Electric Reliability Council of Texas (ERCOT), energy prices are set dynamically to dampen demand shocks. Utilities may also invest in storage technologies to absorb excess capacity during periods of low demand, called load shedding, and contract for supplement generation during periods of high demand, financed through surge pricing. The most common form of storage today is pumped hydro, in which water is pumped into an elevated reservoir—often at an existing dam—during periods of low demand and released to power turbines that generate electricity during periods of high demand.

Another strategy for managing supply and demand fluctuations is to extend transmission grids across regions with different supply and demand characteristics. One of the major costs of our shift to renewables will be the construction of additional transmission capacity.

The introduction of renewable energy sources adds complexity to the management of load on the electrical grid. Wind and solar sources are intermittent. In some regions, periods of high wind and solar intensity correspond with peak demand. This is especially true in the tropics, where maximum solar intensity matches the time of highest demand to power air-conditioning. In West Texas, where both wind and solar energy are abundant, the pattern of generation overlaps favorably. Wind generation is strongest in the mornings and evenings, while solar is most productive during midday. But when generation from wind and solar doesn't match easily with patterns of local demand, grid operators face a complex load-matching challenge.

Renewable power generators typically negotiate long-term sales contracts called power purchase agreements (PPAs) that fix the price at which they will sell their power to the grid operator for a period ranging from ten to twenty-five years. PPAs also commonly require grid operators to purchase *all* of the energy that renewable installations produce. That means that renewable sources increasingly operate as a component of base load, even though they are intermittent. As the share of renewables supplying power to a grid increases, nonrenewable sources are called on to manage supply and demand mismatches. Usually this means relying more heavily on flexible gas- or oil-powered plants. For countries that rely heavily on coal, a growth in renewable energy generation may require that

96 A CONCISE BUSINESS GUIDE TO CLIMATE CHANGE

traditional base-load sources like coal plants be turned on and off to match supply to demand. This intermittent use of base-load supply can degrade efficiency and require additional maintenance.

As the share of renewables in the energy mix increases, the challenges of load matching are also likely to grow. That challenge has led governments and industry to invest in new storage technologies. One possibility is to use grid-scale battery storage to supplement existing pumped hydro capacity. Battery technologies are improving, and many grid-scale facilities are already being installed. A second possibility is to generate non-CO_2-emitting green fuels that can be used to run conventional peaking plants. This possibility, along with the need of commercial airlines to find a green alternative to conventional kerosene fuels, has drawn attention to possibilities for using no-CO_2 green ammonia to generate electricity and produce green kerosene.

The Cost and Benefits of Renewables

Despite the challenges of intermittency, renewable energy sources have important advantages. Disconnected from gas or oil markets, the resulting energy prices are generally insulated from economic or commodity shocks. Renewables can also be produced domestically in most countries, reducing concerns about the role of energy in geopolitical conflicts. One of the most attractive advantages of renewables, however, is that they are increasingly inexpensive when compared to fossil fuels.

To compare the price of electricity across different fuels and technologies, we use a standardized measure called the levelized cost of electricity (LCOE). The LCOE combines both the capital expenditure of building a generation facility and the fuel and operating expenditures needed to produce electricity. In general, renewable generation tends to have higher up-front capital costs of

TABLE 5-1

Levelized cost of electricity for different energy sources

	Nuclear	Coal	Gas	Solar PV	Onshore wind
Capital expenditure ($/MWh)	61	52	9	27	30
Operating expenses ($/MWh)	26	29	30	6	7
Capacity factor (%)	90	85	87	29	41
Levelized cost of electricity ($/MWh)	88	83	40	36	40

Source: U.S. Energy Information Administration, Annual Energy Outlook 2022, U.S. Department of Energy, March 2022, https://www.eia.gov/outlooks/aeo/electricity_generation.php.

gas but dramatically lower operating costs. (See table 5-1.) The capital costs are measured per MW of power. The operating costs are measured per MWh of energy. By spreading the capital costs across the entire lifetime of each source of electricity and then adding operating costs, we can estimate the total average cost per KWh of energy generated.

In order to allocate the capital costs correctly, we also need to factor in the amount of time a generating facility will actually be producing electricity. This is called the capacity factor. Renewables tend to have lower-capacity factors than fossil fuels. The capacity factor for coal is typically around 85 percent, whereas for solar, it is closer to 30 percent. This means that the capital costs for renewables projects have to be spread across fewer total MWh of energy produced, raising their LCOE. Taken together, including capital and operating expenses, new wind and solar generation are less expensive than coal and nuclear, and about the same price as gas generation.

This sort of LCOE calculation allows us to compare the cost of different generation technologies, but it has limitations. First, it is an assessment of current technology. Wind turbines installed five to ten years ago were less efficient, and they are still operating today. Second, old coal and gas plants for which the initial capital investment has long been amortized can produce electricity at close to their operating cost. Finally, and most importantly, the LCOE imposes no cost for the intermittency of renewable sources. In reality, intermittent sources increase the challenge of load matching and therefore the cost of meeting demand. Despite these limitations, the declining cost of renewables, and the likely continuation of that trend into the future, has meant that solar or wind are often the most economically advantageous technologies to meet new electricity demand.

Early solar and wind generation was significantly more expensive than conventional fossil fuels. In order to encourage its use, governments around the world subsidized renewable sources by allowing them to sell their electricity into the grid at higher costs. This was done through feed-in tariffs that were set to match the cost of different renewables technology. Because the feed-in tariffs locked in elevated offtake rates for many years—most set prices for twenty years—renewables producers were able to use those contracts as collateral to finance wind and solar installation. From roughly the late 2010s, as the price of power from wind and solar energy prices reached parity with gas, most countries that had used feed-in tariffs to encourage renewable generation shifted to competitive auctioning based on PPAs. And continued improvements in wind and solar technology and manufacturing imply that the future costs of renewables are likely to fall significantly below the price of fossil fuels.

The rapid shift in the price of renewable sources of energy emphasizes the critical role of innovation in the climate transition. Countries and companies are investing in a wide range of promising new energy technologies, beyond wind and solar, that may further transform our energy mix. These include enhanced geothermal generation, small modular reactors, fusion generation, and a range of plant-based fuels that could displace fossil fuels. A breakthrough in any one of these technologies has the potential to fundamentally upend the economics of energy generation. For now, wind and solar are the workhorse energy sources for decarbonization, but that may not always be the case.

The prospect of abundant and inexpensive renewable energy has driven interest and investment in using that energy to solve other climate problems. We could synthesize green hydrocarbons that might help to decarbonize other parts of the economy. These include sustainable aviation fuel for air transport, green bunker fuel for shipping, and even green hydrogen. Low-cost renewable energy might also be used to power other climate solutions, including carbon removal technologies like direct carbon capture. Already solar energy is being used to power desalination plans and synthesize green ammonia for fertilizer. We as a society have never experienced economic development powered by abundant, truly inexpensive energy, and it will be exciting to see what opportunities that might create, especially for the populations of developing countries.

Concluding Thoughts

Even as solar and wind have become cost-competitive with fossil fuel energy sources, important challenges remain in decarbonizing our electrical grids. First, major investments in new renewable generation will have to be made. And for the near term, at least, the capital costs of those projects are likely to be significantly higher than the costs of fossil fuel generation. That high initial investment means that renewables projects depend on the cost of capital. Protracted higher interest rates would create obstacles to building out necessary renewables. Meanwhile, legacy fossil fuel facilities have long life spans, and their capital costs have often been paid off long in the past. This suggests that renewables are going to be more attractive in developing countries with growing power needs than in advanced economies with stable or even declining energy needs. Managing the sunsetting of legacy fossil fuel generation in sync with the build-out of renewable capacity will have to be carefully coordinated. To the extent that incumbent generators have built political connections and influence, they may push against projects to phase out fossil fuel generation.

The second challenge relates to our capacity to build cost-effective electricity storage, and the choice of storage technologies to pursue. As with many areas of decarbonization, there is significant risk and uncertainty associated with our choice of storage technology. At the time of writing, the most cost-effective grid-scale battery technology was lithium-ion chemistry—the same that runs our EVs and cell phones. But we are also in a moment of intensive research into alternative chemistries and storage strategies, and those new approaches may ultimately prove to be the winners. Given the scale of investments in these new technologies, poor choices could lead to significant financial costs.

Finally, the challenges associated with building out necessary new transmission are daunting. Historically, we have built our industry near sources of power—be it near rivers for hydropower, or near coal mines. For the most part, those industrial zones have remained where they were founded. Yet the most abundant and cheapest renewable energy sources today are typically located elsewhere. Lands blessed with abundant solar, wind, and hydropower are often far from where we have traditionally consumed that power. Yet building transmission between regions of production and consumption is likely to be challenging. Not only are transmission lines expensive, they also often require that governments seize private property to build them. This creates powerful local resistance that can in turn squelch such projects.

An alternative scenario is to relocate our most energy-intensive industries to where the abundant renewables sources are. That could call for shifting some of European industry to southern Spain and western Morocco, for moving American steel and chemicals plants to Texas, and for relocating Chinese industry to take advantage of abundant winds in the Gobi Desert. Such an approach, if we pursue it, would profoundly reorganize our industrial society, creating new winners and losers.

CHAPTER 6

POLICY RESPONSE TO CLIMATE CHANGE

This chapter explores the global policy response to climate change and then focuses in on the specific approaches adopted in Europe, the United States, and China. In the global context, it introduces the United Nations Intergovernmental Panel on Climate Change (IPCC), the Kyoto Protocol, and the Paris Agreement. The nature of our global response to climate change has shifted in important ways over the past decade. Whereas the Kyoto Protocol is often described as a top-down approach to reducing emissions, the Paris Agreement shifted to a more voluntary, bottom-up approach. At the national level, that change was reflected in a shift toward economic policies that emphasized new subsidies and protections for domestic green industry.

Historically, the greatest obstacle to addressing climate change has been coordination. The problem was that a stable global climate was a public good. In economics, that term has a particular meaning: it is used to describe goods or services to which all have access, and for which the use by one does not reduce the use by others—a characteristic economists refer to as "nonrivalry." Lighthouses are a classic example. For all of the lighthouses' benefits, economists had noted that public goods of this kind tended to be under-provided in society. The reason, they concluded, had to do with a problem of coordination. So long as reducing GHG emissions required additional investments and costs, then no single country had an incentive to respond to the challenge first. In fact, the optimal strategy was to shirk and let others bear the burden of emissions reduction. But if everyone did this, nothing would happen. It was only by working together that we could reduce emissions in a way that did not penalize some countries and make free riders of others. Fortunately, world leaders immediately following World War II had formed the United Nations with exactly this sort of global coordination challenge in mind. The UN remains the key institution for coordinating our response to climate change today.

An adequate response to climate change faces two other challenges that also had to be addressed. First, the costs of climate change in the form of economic and ecological disruption would primarily be borne by future generations. That meant that current political constituencies would have to take action for benefits that would mostly accrue not to them, but to their descendants. How those interests should be represented today raised issues related to intergenerational justice. Critical to understanding those future costs was a scientific consensus around the likely future scenarios of climate change and their impacts on future society.

The second problem related to poorer countries in the Global South that had contributed very little to climate change, but that would need to fundamentally restructure their societies to limit GHG emissions. An equitable response to the climate crisis would require the advanced industrialized countries to support what came to be called a just transition. This implied that industrialized countries would take on greater responsibility for having contributed heavily to climate change and provide financial and technological support for developing countries to manage their response. It also increasingly extended to include support for adaptation measures in developing countries and compensation for damage and disruption caused by climate change.

The UN Framework

Climate change came into focus as a policy topic at the United Nations in the early 1990s, after the end of the Cold War, and the UN remains the primary institutional setting for coordinating how we address the challenge. However, the nature of that response has shifted fairly dramatically since then. We can distinguish two phases. The first was the approach adopted under the Kyoto Protocol, from 1997 to roughly 2015. The Kyoto approach has been described as top-down, with global coordination around emissions reduction targets, along with carbon emissions trading and enforcement. From 2015, our climate response has been dictated by the terms of the Paris Agreement. The Paris Agreement has been described as a bottom-up approach, in which countries set their own desired carbon emissions goals, while agreeing to common standards of accounting and transparency. We look at both approaches in more detail later in this chapter.

Our initial template for a response to the climate crisis came from the Montreal Protocol, a successful international effort to limit the emission of ozone-destroying chlorofluorocarbons (CFCs) and halogenated hydrocarbons (halons) that were commonly used as refrigerants, accelerants, and solvents. Ozone absorbs ultraviolet radiation from the Sun, providing protection for the Earth's surface, and CFCs and halons were destroying that ozone. Negotiated in the context of the United Nations, the 1987 Montreal Protocol set a reduction trajectory and introduced a cap-and-trade system to achieve emissions reductions efficiently. It also established a multilateral fund to help poorer countries adjust. It was, by many accounts, the most effective international agreement ever implemented. When the Kyoto Protocol was being drafted, the Montreal Protocol was very much on the minds of its designers.

Concerns about climate justice were part of the response to climate change from the very beginning. The UN Framework Convention on Climate Change (UNFCCC) that established the way in which we continue to address climate justice today recognized that both rich and poor signatories shared "common but differentiated responsibilities and respective capabilities" to address climate change (Article 3.1). In practice that meant that developed countries had greater responsibilities. This principle was embedded at the heart of the Kyoto Protocol and taken up again in the Paris Agreement.

The UN Framework Convention on Climate Change

A global response to climate change emerged soon after the fall of the Soviet Union. With the Cold War divisiveness seemingly in the past, 180 nations gathered in 1992 at the Earth Summit organized by the United Nations in Rio de Janeiro with a goal to address a broad range of ecological problems, including pollution, water safety, and protection for the oceans, as well as climate change.

Out of the Earth Summit emerged a number of important initiatives, including the Commission on Sustainable Development, the Convention on Biological Diversity, and the UNFCCC. The UNFCCC, with a secretariat in Bonn, Germany, was ratified in 1994. Its organizing body, called the Conference of Parties (COP), was constituted of all the signatory countries. The COP met annually. At its fourth meeting, in Kyoto, Japan, members agreed to additions to the UNFCCC that provided a specific strategy to address climate change. The approach, called the Kyoto Protocol, would only be ratified if countries accounting for at least 55 percent of global emissions signed onto it. Even though the United States, the largest GHG emitter at the time, did not ratify the Kyoto Protocol, enough other nations did, and it went into effect in 1997.

While climate policy is set through negotiations in the context of the UNFCCC, the UN also established a body to inform UN member states on the state of research on climate change. In 1988, even before the creation of the UNFCCC, the UN Environment Programme and the World Meteorological Organization created a joint initiative called the Intergovernmental Panel on Climate Change (IPCC). The IPCC is headquartered in Geneva and governed by 195 member states. Its mandate is to undertake periodic reviews of the state of science on climate, and to publish reports on its findings every six to seven years. Reports of the IPCC help to inform policy-making within the UNFCCC, although they remain organizationally independent. The most recent *Sixth Assessment Report*, published in 2021–2022, led the UNFCCC to set a global policy target of 1.5°C temperature rise above preindustrial levels at its COP26 meeting in Glasgow, Scotland.

The Kyoto Protocol

The Kyoto Protocol was intended as an evolving set of standards. It set a goal of a 5 percent reduction in GHG emissions below a 1990 baseline for the first commitment period, which was set for the period 2008–2012. Different countries and regions committed to different targets, depending on their capabilities. The European Union, for example, committed to an ambitious 8 percent reduction below 1990 levels, while Canada and Japan committed to a 6 percent reduction,

108 A CONCISE BUSINESS GUIDE TO CLIMATE CHANGE

and Russia set a target of 0 percent. In principle, the Kyoto Protocol also included an enforcement mechanism, which mostly amounted to a threat to increase future reductions in case countries fell short of past targets. For the second commitment period, set for 2013–2020, signatories committed to reduce emissions by at least 18 percent, on average, below 1990 levels.

The Kyoto Protocol was attentive to concerns about climate justice. In the agreement, the industrialized countries, designated as "Annex I" signatories, committed to undertaking the bulk of emissions reductions. The 133 developing-country Kyoto Protocol signatories did not commit to emissions reductions during the first commitment period, on the understanding that they had not primarily caused the problem. Concern that large developing countries like China and India did not have to commit to reductions drove some of the resistance to ratification in the United States. In 2001, the UNFCCC created the Adaptation Fund that would support climate-related projects in developing countries.

Concern about climate justice was also built into the structure of Kyoto's cap-and-trade scheme. Modeled on the Montreal Protocol governing ozone-depleting chemicals, the Kyoto Protocol included "flexibility mechanisms" that permitted emissions trading among signatories. The goal was to reduce the overall cost of meeting the set targets. Countries for which the cost of reduction was high, for example, could purchase emissions permits, called assigned amount units (AAUs), from countries that were able to reduce their emissions at lower cost.

To this basic system of emissions trading, Kyoto added two additional mechanisms that would help to address fairness questions related to the green transition in developing and middle-income countries. One scheme, called joint implementation (JI), granted carbon offsets called emission reduction units (ERUs) for investments that reduced emissions among Annex I signatories of the

POLICY RESPONSE TO CLIMATE CHANGE **109**

Kyoto Protocol. A second scheme, called the Clean Development Mechanism (CDM), awarded emissions offsets called certified emissions reductions (CERs) for projects in developing countries that durably reduced carbon emissions. Like all offset schemes, the JI and CDM projects had to be certified in order to be valid, and the UN recognized dozens of crediting agencies around the world to undertake this certification. The idea was that the sale of CERs and ERUs to Annex I Kyoto signatories to help them meet their emissions reductions targets would provide a mechanism to finance emissions reduction in developing countries. During the late 2000s and early 2010s, a first wave of renewable energy projects in developing countries earned ERUs as part of their revenue stream.

For all of the careful attention to design, the Kyoto Protocol suffered important setbacks. Most importantly, the United States failed to ratify the treaty, partly over objections that poorer countries like China and India were not required to make commitments. In advance of the second commitment period, from 2012 to 2020, Japan, Russia, and Canada also withdrew from the Kyoto Protocol.

Further, as negotiations for the second commitment period were underway, the ambitious flexibility mechanisms at the heart of the Kyoto Protocol fell under suspicion. In 2010, critics noted that over half of all CERs awarded for CDM projects were going to manufacturers of refrigerant chemicals that committed to reduce the emissions of a powerful GHG called HFC-23 that was associated with their production. Most of the refrigerant manufacturers were located in India and China. Amid suspicion that the CERs associated with HFC-23 removal were creating perverse incentives for refrigerant manufacturers—manufacturers were producing *more* HFC-23 in order to claim CERs—the UN limited how many CERs manufacturers could sell. The EU, which had enacted its own Emissions Trading System intended to work closely with the Kyoto cap-and-trade scheme (see the discussion of the European response to

110   A CONCISE BUSINESS GUIDE TO CLIMATE CHANGE

climate change later in this chapter), stopped recognizing any CERs that derived from HFC-23 projects.

Finally, the Kyoto Protocol was unusually hermetic in its approach. It did not link negotiated emissions reductions directly to scientific findings of the IPCC. It also did not include many actors that could have been important partners in GHG emissions reduction. Regional, urban, and business interests were mostly excluded from the negotiations. Even as countries negotiated bilateral climate accords—including critically between China and the United States—the Kyoto Protocol maintained a focus on multilateral negotiations that seemed to drag on without sufficiently ambitious results. Efforts to create an enforcement mechanism for signatories, for example, never came to fruition. And the prices of tradable GHG permits—AAUs, CERs, and ERUs—*declined* over the course of the first commitment period. Low and falling prices for GHG emissions seemed to mirror low and falling ambition for emissions reduction.

The Paris Agreement

Even as UNFCCC negotiators lamented the lack of ambition of the Kyoto Protocol, a new strategy was emerging that would displace it. The idea was introduced in the 2009 Copenhagen meeting of the Conference of Parties (COP15) and ultimately codified in the Paris Agreement negotiated at the 21st Conference of Parties (COP21) in 2015. The approach has been described as a bottom-up approach, reflecting a relatively hands-off, decentralized strategy of coordination around GHG emissions reduction. The new Paris Agreement would replace the Kyoto Protocol once the second commitment period ended, in 2020.

Under the terms of the new agreement, 186 signatory countries announced intended GHG emissions reduction targets for 2030, called nationally determined contributions (NDCs). The NDCs were the heart of the Paris Agreement, and most of the largest emitters have also declared net-zero target dates—typically by 2050 or 2060. Unlike under the Kyoto Protocol, these targets were neither binding nor negotiated. And NDCs often used different baseline years, making them difficult to compare directly with each other (see table 6-1). Signatories also agreed to a specific target for global temperature rise, not to exceed 2°C above preindustrial levels, with China committing to peak carbon emissions in 2030, after which they will decline. This kind of science-based target had not been a part of the Kyoto Protocol mechanism. At the COP26 meeting in Glasgow in 2021, as the preliminary findings of the IPCC *Sixth Assessment Report* were made public, signatories further agreed to pursue efforts to meet a 1.5°C target.

The new approach seemed to embody a profound contradiction. On the one hand, the new agreement seemed to lack teeth: signatories to the Paris Agreement would set their own voluntary emissions reduction targets, without any enforcement mechanism. On the other hand, a very large number of countries, including both industrialized and developing nations, announced ambitious emissions reduction targets that, if achieved, would go a long way to limiting the impact of climate change. (See table 6-1.)

While the substance of national emissions targets was set voluntarily, Paris Agreement signatories committed to a set of procedural rules that provided transparency and tracking for their progress toward meeting those targets. This set of procedural standards was defined in the Paris Agreement Rulebook and covered four main areas. First, it defined a standard set of carbon accounting guidelines for anthropogenic emissions and removals, including how tradable emissions permits would be recorded. Second, signatories agreed to participate in a global stock-take in which they reported on their current emissions levels, their intended path forward, and

TABLE 6-1

Nationally determined contributions of major emitters

	2030 target	Baseline year		Net zero date	Gases covered
United States	-50%	2005		2050	All GHG
EU	-55%	1990		2050	All GHG
Japan	-46%	2013		2050	All GHG
China	Emissions peak in 2030			2060	Only CO_2
India	-45%	2005		2070	Not specified
IPCC global	-45%	2019		2050–2060	All GHG

the policy tools they proposed to use to get there. Those would be incorporated into a new set of national climate commitments announced in 2025. Third, they agreed to an enhanced transparency framework, including biennial reporting for developed economies and common reporting standards. Finally, they agreed to announce updated NDCs in 2030 for the subsequent five-year implementation period.

The Paris Agreement also differed from Kyoto in its openness to "nonparty stakeholders," including municipal and state governments as well as companies. The 2016 COP22 meeting in Marrakesh announced the formation of the Marrakesh Partnership for Global Climate Action (MPGCA) with the goal of formalizing the participation of nonstate actors. The MPGCA publicized the climate commitments and achievements of nonstate actors. It established the role of national climate champions, business leaders at the forefront of climate change who could advocate on behalf of emissions reduction activities. And it convened regional climate action summits at which state and nonstate actors could meet. Together, these efforts recognized the critical role of nonstate actors in implementing the changes that would be needed to reduce GHG emissions. For the first time, global climate negotiations and forums were open to business.

The Paris Agreement also sought to address concerns about climate justice. Unlike under Kyoto, where climate justice was integrated into the cap-and-trade flexibility mechanism, the provisions for climate justice under the Paris Agreement took the form of national pledges to make payments to developing countries. Industrialized nations that signed the Paris Agreement also committed to providing $100 billion to developing countries for climate adaptation and mitigation. By 2020, less than 20 percent of those funds had been provided. At the 2022 COP27 meeting in Cairo, Egypt, the advanced industrialized nations agreed to create a fund to compensate least developed countries for loss and damage due to climate change. Critics have noted that potential donor countries were slow to provide actual financing.

Regional Approaches to Climate Change

Historically, US and European approaches to climate change have been quite different. Even within Europe, national responses have differed significantly. These differences have created one of the major challenges that confront global firms working to decarbonize their operations. European automakers, for example, face a 2035 deadline set by the European Union to end all sales of internal combustion engines. Yet these firms also sell in the United States and China, where such a ban is unlikely. Navigating these different market standards may require that companies pursue differentiated approaches to meeting their decarbonization targets.

Two factors primarily have driven differences in national responses. The first is the fossil fuel endowment of a country. Nearly systematically, countries with greater fossil fuel endowments have tended to be slower to respond to climate change. The United States, for example, with vast oil and coal reserves, has been less aggressive in addressing climate change than oil-poor Europe. The oil- and coal-rich countries also typically have the greatest partisan divide over the causes and response to climate change. Countries like France and Japan, which have very few domestic fossil fuel resources, moved early to develop climate-friendly energy sources, with special focus on nuclear. Today, France already generates two-thirds of its electricity from nuclear power.

The second important factor is the nature of their political system. For countries with political systems that favor two dominant political parties, like the United States, climate change has tended to be relegated as a political focus. Political parties in these two-party systems tend to tack toward the median voter, the one in the middle of the political spectrum, and that voter has not historically been attentive to climate change. For countries that encourage competition of multiple parties, as in much of continental Europe, green environmental parties appeared in the 1980s and 1990s that became standard bearers for addressing climate change. In Germany, for example, the Green Party has become a de facto kingmaker in parliamentary elections: either major party, Christian Democratic Union (CDU) and Social Democratic Party (SPD) has had to form coalitions with the Greens in order to establish a ruling majority. The Greens have used their wedge power to push aggressively for renewable energy sources.

Given their importance in the global climate response, we focus in more detail on US, EU, and Chinese climate policies.

US Response to Climate Change

From a historical perspective, the partisanship of US attitudes to climate change is new. Historically, environmental protection has been a bipartisan issue in the United States. The landmark 1970 Clean Air Act and the 1970 Environmental Protection Act were both passed by the conservative Nixon administration with support from the political left. At the time, the United States was a global leader in air- and water-quality regulation.

With the end of the Cold War, as policy makers focused on a global response to climate change, US support for a response emerged primarily on the political left. From that moment, the growing political partisanship of climate change as a policy issue precluded a unified national response. Hence, the United States negotiated the Kyoto Protocol under the Clinton administration in 1995, but then failed to ratify it. The Obama administration signed onto the Paris Agreement, in 2015, but the Trump administration pulled the country out of the agreement. The Biden administration subsequently rejoined, and then the second Trump administration pulled out again. In this partisan context, US responses to climate change from the mid-1990s to the mid-2020s were partial and fragmented.

Despite the political disagreement, four main policies have driven the US response to climate change. The first of these is the Corporate Average Fuel Economy (CAFE) standard that sets fuel efficiency requirements for automobile manufacturers. Introduced in 1974, it was intended for an entirely different purpose—to reduce US dependence on foreign oil in the wake of the first oil shock. Nonetheless, as the fuel efficiency of automobiles increased, that reduced the carbon dioxide emissions from the transportation sector.

A second policy has been to extend the responsibility of the Environmental Protection Agency (EPA) under the Clean Air Act to regulate carbon dioxide as a pollutant. This policy was enabled by a 2009 decision of the US Supreme Court finding that CO_2 was indeed a pollutant. Based on this ruling, the Obama administration created a Clean Power Plan (CPP) that would have shut down the majority of American coal power plants. The Trump administration shelved the CPP, and the Supreme Court in 2022 raised questions about the EPA's authority to regulate CO_2 under existing laws.

The third approach has been to rely on regional and local initiatives to drive policy toward climate change. In 2006, the California Air Resources Board created America's first GHG cap-and-trade system to achieve emissions reduction targets set by the state. In 2015, it linked the California carbon market with markets in Quebec and Ontario, allowing California companies to purchase cheaper Canadian carbon offsets to meet their emissions reduction targets. In 2009, ten Northeast and mid-Atlantic states set a similar emissions cap for the power sector and created a regional carbon trading system called the Regional Greenhouse Gas Initiative (RGGI, pronounced "reggie").

Finally, the United States has periodically provided input subsidies for renewable energies. In 1992, for example, the federal government introduced a production tax credit for wind turbine installations. These were short-term tax incentives but were frequently extended. In 2022, Congress passed two major renewable energy incentive bills—the CHIPS and Science Act, and the Inflation Reduction Act— that allocated a combined $350 billion in subsidies to research and production of renewable technologies.

Partly as a result of these programs, US GHG emissions peaked in 2005 and began to decline. Yet the most important contributor in that reduction was a shift away from coal and toward natural gas in thermal energy generation. The shift in fuel source was driven by low gas prices resulting from discovery and exploitation of new and abundant shale gas resources in North Dakota, Texas, Michigan, Pennsylvania, and Ohio. Because coal produces twice as much CO_2 emissions per energy produced as does natural gas (methane), shifting fuel sources resulted in a decline in US GHG emissions.

European Response to Climate Change

Within Europe, the European Union has coordinated member state responses to climate change. But that common front hides a range of national responses. The EU committed to an 8 percent reduction in emissions below 1990 levels during the first commitment period of the Kyoto Protocol, from 2008 to 2012, for example, but the burden of reduction was born differently by different EU member countries depending on their circumstances. France, which already heavily relied on nuclear power, committed only to stabilize its emissions at current levels. Germany, in which the Green Party had become a powerful voice in national politics, committed to a 21 percent reduction. Poorer member states like Portugal and Greece were granted scope to increase their emissions by up to 25 percent.

Europe's Kyoto commitments were applied through a cap-and-trade system for carbon emissions called the European Union Emissions Trading System (EU ETS) that covered Europe's major emitters, including power generators and energy-intensive steel and chemical producers. EU ETS emissions permits were distributed to these companies based on their historical emissions levels, with 1990 set as the base year. Under the scheme, producers would have to redeem permits to cover their annual emissions. If they did not have enough permits, they could purchase them from others. The goal was to ensure that producers with the lowest cost of reduction would reduce more while generating revenue by selling their excess permits. The scheme also linked to the international emissions trading market created by the Kyoto Protocol. This meant that European companies could purchase carbon offsets generated by renewables projects in developing countries under the CDM.

The legacy of the EU ETS was mixed. On the one hand, it succeeded in creating the world's first functioning carbon trading market. As such, it would become the template for later carbon trading markets around the world. On the other hand, the price of carbon traded on the EU ETS remained low, suggesting that it was not having a dramatic effect holding down emissions.

Even though the price of carbon remained low, European GHG emissions fell significantly over the first two commitment periods of the Kyoto Protocol, from 2008 to 2020. GHG emissions declined from 5.2 gigatons CO_2 to 3.7 gigatons CO_2 over that period. Much of that decline came from Germany, where emissions had peaked in 1979 and by 2020 had declined by half. The story of Germany's success in reducing emissions had very little to do with the Kyoto Protocol, however. It was, instead, the product of Germany's environmental movement.

In 1974, OPEC organized to restrict global oil production, and Germany's energy prices spiked. In response, the German government launched ambitious new coal and nuclear programs to reduce Germany's energy dependence. German environmentalists protested these projects and, in particular, succeeded in blocking the construction of new nuclear facilities. These protests gave birth to Germany's Green Party, which for the first time joined a ruling coalition with the center-left SPD in 1990. Their very first policy was to push for renewable energy subsidies in the form of feed-in tariffs (FITs), in the hope that wind and solar power installations could displace coal and nuclear generation. By 2020, wind, solar, and biomass together accounted for over half of Germany's electricity generation. The cost was born primarily by German households, which frequently paid twice what their French counterparts did for electricity.

In 2015, when the European Union signed the Paris Agreement to hold down the global temperature increase to 2°C, it pledged to decrease GHG emissions 40 percent by 2030 and 80 percent by 2050. In 2019, the EU dramatically increased its ambition. It pledged to reduce emissions 55 percent by 2030, a policy referred to as "Fit for 55," and to achieve carbon neutrality by 2050. Its formula for carbon

POLICY RESPONSE TO CLIMATE CHANGE

neutrality included 90 percent GHG emissions reductions and a further 10 percent GHG capture and sequestration. It would achieve these goals through a range of sectoral policies referred to collectively as the Green Deal. These included higher emissions standards for automobiles, ambitious targets for efficient buildings and recycling, and support for technology investments in green hydrogen and carbon sequestration.

These policies were implemented within a new European climate framework that had three pillars. First, the 2021 European Climate Law gave the EU climate commitments under the Paris Agreement the status of law. This meant governments could be sued if they were not pursuing policies consistent with these goals. Second, the 2021 Corporate Sustainability Reporting Directive (CSRD) required 18,000 firms and local governments to report their CO_2 emissions. Third, the EU announced the Carbon Border Adjustment Mechanism (CBAM) that would tax the import of energy-intensive products based on their carbon emissions. Initially, the program would target the Scope 1 emissions of energy-intensive imports like steel, fertilizer, and cement.

CBAM has been the focus of considerable global concern. The policy was intended to ensure that European firms subject to the costs of the EU ETS would not face a disadvantage relative to competitors importing from countries without restrictions on carbon emissions. It also faced special criticism from developing countries. Their governments argue that CBAM is a form of protectionism, designed to ensure that Europe's own firms will enjoy an advantage over foreign producers. Some have suggested that CBAM is inconsistent with the international trading standards laid out by the World Trade Organization. Yet other developing countries see it as an opportunity. They believe that CBAM may support green industrial strategies in countries that have especially abundant renewable energy sources.

As this brief treatment suggests, the scope of Europe's policy response to climate change is vast and evolving, with detailed technology and business road maps for the major emitting sectors: electricity, transportation, housing, agriculture, and industry.

Green Industrial Policy in China

China's response to climate change differed from those in the United States and Europe in part because it was still at a relatively early stage of economic development when it began. In the early 2000s, as international attention increasingly focused on the climate threat, China was experiencing rapid growth driven by an export-led economic strategy, with high projected energy demands. For the foreseeable future, that energy would come primarily from coal. Between 2005 and 2024, China's coal-fired power capacity grew fourfold, from 300 GW to 1,200 GW.[1] Coal is a potent source of carbon dioxide, and China's CO_2 emissions also quadrupled over this time, from 3 billion tons per year in 2000 to nearly 12 billion tons per year in 2024. With total global emissions at 40 billion tons at that time, China had become the world's largest GHG emitter, with nearly a third of global emissions.

However, this coal-powered energy spree did not stop China from engaging around climate change. In 1997, China joined as a signatory to the Kyoto Protocol with the status of a developing country. This meant it was not required to reduce its emissions during the first commitment period (2008–2012). As a signatory, however, it was able to receive CDM credits and associated payments for renewable energy projects developed in collaboration with European and US renewables generators. This mechanism drove an influx of wind energy development projects, and by 2012, China had a remarkable 64 GW of wind production capacity certified for CDM credits.

POLICY RESPONSE TO CLIMATE CHANGE 121

What followed was a series of policies that restricted imports and provided domestic subsidies to promote development of renewable energy. The 11th Five-Year Plan, covering 2006–2010, set a renewable energy target of 10GW by 2010. In 2009, China introduced a wind-generation FIT inspired by the German renewable subsidy strategy that drove a surge in new investment in domestic generation. Meanwhile, increasingly restrictive local content requirements led domestic firms to build technical skills in turbine and blade design and manufacturing. These efforts were supported by government-sponsored research on new energy sources, and R&D tax credits for firms undertaking wind innovation.

Whereas wind production in China was oriented primarily toward the local energy market, solar manufacturing was initially focused on exports, mostly to Europe to meet demand driven by solar FITs. But when the global financial crisis and Eurozone crisis led to a pullback of the European subsidies, in 2009–2012, all of that changed. With falling exports, China's solar PV manufacturers were suffering, and Beijing stepped in to provide support in the form of domestic PV demand. The 2009 "Golden Sun" initiative, for example, provided supports for rooftop solar, and regional governments were given specific renewable energy targets. As China's PV panel manufacturers consolidated, they built scale and know-how, and the price of panels began to fall rapidly. By 2018, both solar and wind generation had reached price parity with incumbent fossil fuel generation.

The third pillar of China's renewable strategy focused on electric vehicles (EVs). Chinese auto producers had struggled to break into mature auto markets in Europe and the United States, and a focus on EVs seemed to offer a way to leapfrog existing technologies and establish a technology advantage. Beginning in 2010, when China's State Council identified EVs as a "strategic emerging industry," Beijing began providing supports to build capability in EVs. Initially, EV buyers received government subsidies. As that became too costly,

122   A CONCISE BUSINESS GUIDE TO CLIMATE CHANGE

Beijing shifted to a combination of fleet efficiency and new EV sales targets—policies that it copied from initiatives developed to support EV sales in California. By 2024, fully a third of all new cars sold in China were electric vehicles. As with solar and wind technologies, Chinese firms were able to use scale, new technology, and lower wages to bring down battery and vehicle costs nearly to price parity with existing internal combustion engine vehicles. Both the United States and Europe responded by imposing import tariffs on Chinese EVs.

China's strategy of treating green technologies as a focus of concerted industrial policy was quickly copied around the world. India raised tariffs on Chinese imports, provided subsidies for wind and solar generation, and launched an ambitious target of generating half of all its electricity from renewables by 2030. The United States saw Chinese dominance of new green technologies as an economic threat and responded with a mix of tariffs and subsidies to support domestic producers and supply chains. Europe followed suit with new subsidies for green technologies, backed by tariffs and CBAM. In this new world of green competition fueled by active state industrial policy, the major economies of the world increasingly saw decarbonization as an essential pillar of their broader economic strategy.

Concluding Thoughts

Against the backdrop of the Paris Agreement, the logic and context of national responses to climate change were shifting. Whereas the early Kyoto Protocol had relied on top-down pressure to drive national emissions reduction, Paris Agreement signatories increasingly saw their emissions reduction goals as part of a broader industrial policy focused on green technologies. In the context of a green economic transition, countries with strong technical capabilities in the related technologies were likely to enjoy significant industrial suc-

POLICY RESPONSE TO CLIMATE CHANGE   123

cess. In order to encourage this success, national governments increasingly moved to subsidize domestic renewables technologies and to protect their markets from foreign competition.

In many ways, this new approach to climate policy seemed to turn our theories about decarbonization on their head. Rather than embracing global markets, the world's major economic regions would decarbonize more independently. Rather than seeing climate response as a threat to economic prosperity, developing countries like China, India, and Brazil increasingly saw climate technologies as the key to a new stage of industrial growth. And rather than cooperating to address a common problem, national governments seemed to be competing to get ahead in a new technology race. The result was likely to be less cooperation, but with potentially more rapid progress.

At the heart of this change in approach to climate change has been a fundamental shift in the underlying technologies we will need to address climate change. The main trigger has been a revolution in the energy sector, starting with a precipitous drop in the cost of electricity generation from wind and solar sources. In this sense, new technologies drove new policies and politics around climate change. If and when a new generation of renewable technologies becomes cost competitive—green hydrogen, green steel, deep geothermal, fusion— these are likely to further transform our policy response.

CHAPTER 7

FINAL THOUGHTS

The corporate climate transition will be characterized by risk, disruption, and opportunity. Adaptation paths are unlikely to be linear or highly predictable. In the spring of 2022, I was speaking to the owner of a chain of gas stations in Germany. His firm was contemplating installing electric chargers. But he worried that this large investment might be making a bet on the wrong technology. What if electric vehicles were *not* the future of transportation? Six months later, he wrote me to say that they had opted to install hydrogen pumping stations instead. Had he made the right choice? Was there a correct answer? Executives like this are looking into a blurry future, trying to read how markets and regulations are likely to evolve. If they are prescient, they will enjoy outsized profitability. If they make the wrong call, they may have to write off expensive assets. For industrial sectors in which new investments are measured in billions of dollars, these decisions can have dramatic consequences for the future viability of any firm.

How do executives and boards of directors navigate this sort of uncertainty? Perhaps the most important reminder as firms think through this transition is that they face a set of decisions that involves changes in broader systems. This is true both within the firm, at the sectoral level, and at the level of the global economy. Successfully navigating decarbonization will require that executives re-evaluate the ways in which their own strategies fit within the broader sectoral and economic context. What do I mean by this? Let's begin by looking within the firm.

For the past decade, the standard tool for firms seeking to reduce their carbon emissions was the marginal abatement cost curve (MACC). Typically prepared by consultants, it would enumerate different opportunities to reduce GHG emissions, along with their impact on the bottom line. Some investments would generate net savings—for example, shifting from incandescent to LED lighting also reduced energy demand—while others would come at a net loss. Firms would then move down the MACC: beginning with changes that generated most savings, then moving toward more costly responses. While the details of economic adjustment for each sector might differ, the general approach was mechanical.

Today, that mechanical approach is not enough. The MACC provides a menu of options, but deciding how to choose from the menu requires that executives consider climate abatement in the broader strategic context of the firm. What are the key features of their strategic ecosystem? What are the goals of their customers, suppliers, competitors, and employees? Decarbonization has become a core component of corporate strategy, and the basic imperative that strategy fit context is especially true as firms navigate decarbonization.

One thing that makes this set of strategic calculations challenging is that our response to climate change is likely to restructure the competitive logic of many sectors of the economy. Products that had been commodities may now enjoy greater value added and higher margins.

FINAL THOUGHTS   **127**

New product and process innovations will create new sectoral leaders, and new pricing and profit dynamics. In a world in which renewable sources are abundant and cheap, energy-intensive manufacture may relocate to take advantage of that cost advantage. This means that regions that were left behind in the first industrialization—North Africa, Inner Mongolia, the American Southwest—could become economic hubs in the new industrial revolution. Firms that establish dominance in these new regions and technologies will be able to consolidate new markets and set the structure of future competition.

My former colleague, the great economic historian Alfred Chandler, described the first wave of industrialization in the United States as "ten years of competition, followed by one hundred years of oligopoly." Firms like Ford and DuPont that survived the initial competitive battles went on to dominate twentieth-century industry. This perspective also very much captures the competitive stakes in the green transition today. Firms that successfully navigate this moment of industrial reframing will win a place at the table of a new decarbonized economy. And, as with the first industrialization, the economic rewards from that success are potentially enormous and enduring.

A third and final challenge facing firms that have embarked on the path to decarbonization arises from the shifting geopolitics of trade and investment. For most of the postwar period, countries around the world increasingly integrated with each other through growing flows of trade and investment, under the guidance of global rules set by the General Agreement on Tariffs and Trade and through a web of bilateral investment treaties and trade agreements. At just the moment when businesses are confronting decarbonization, however, that global liberal order also appears to be breaking down. National governments that increasingly see the green transition and renewable technologies as the key to future competitiveness are restricting trade and investments in core technologies. This fragmentation has accompanied a move toward regionally specific climate responses. While Europe focuses on electrification using wind and solar, Japan and South Korea are focused on green hydrogen as a climate-friendly fuel source, and Brazil is exploring green ethanol. And, rather than a global system of carbon trading, we are seeing the emergence of bilateral green agreements that establish the terms on which countries manage green trade and investment.

It seems increasingly likely that our response to climate change will fundamentally change the world. Industries will adopt novel production technologies and relocate close to cheap renewable energy. Regions that were left behind in the first industrialization may thrive in the second. Climate justice will raise questions not just about who will be left behind but also about who will be new winners. For entrepreneurs, this moment offers an extraordinary mix of great potential opportunities married to the most ambitious kind of social purpose. Like the inventors of the early steam engines and communications technologies, bold and fortunate climate entrepreneurs will both build economic empires and safeguard human society.

The exact script for how they do this has yet to be written. But what has become increasingly clear is that the most important ideas and technologies that will guide us through this transition will be invented in and deployed by the global business community. As we have seen, governments have important roles to play in guiding this process, but ultimately the largest share of responsibility and rewards will rest on our managerial class. MBA programs globally train a quarter of a million managers each year. This is the moment when we get to see whether this massive investment in business leadership will pay off. Judging from the students and executives I meet in the classroom, and the entrepreneurship I see in the field, my guess is that it will prove to have been one of the most important investments in climate mitigation that we as a society have made.

GLOSSARY

additionality   A principle that ensures carbon offset projects result in additional carbon reductions that would not have occurred without the project.

adiabatic cooling   The process of cooling due to a lowering of air pressure caused by volume expansion. When air rises, as when it must pass over a mountain range, the lower air pressure at higher altitude causes the air to get colder due to adiabatic cooling.

albedo   The measure of the reflectivity of the Earth's surface, with higher albedo indicating more reflection of solar radiation. Clouds and arctic ice cover both have high albedo, reflecting solar radiation back into space, and helping to cool the Earth.

Annex I countries   In the context of the Kyoto Protocol, Annex I countries included the industrialized nations that committed to greenhouse gas emissions reduction. Non–Annex I countries were primarily developing countries that were not subject to mandatory emission reduction targets.

anthracite   A hard, high-carbon coal that burns with little smoke. Because it burns cleanly, it was especially attractive for commercial and home heating.

GLOSSARY

anthropogenic forcing Human activities that influence the climate, such as emissions of greenhouse gases.

assigned amount units (AAUs) Carbon dioxide emission allowances allocated to countries under the Kyoto Protocol. AAUs could be traded among Annex I countries to meet their emissions targets.

Atlantic Meridional Overturning Circulation (AMOC) A large system of ocean currents that circulates warm, salty water from the tropics to the North Atlantic, and cold Arctic waters back toward the tropics. The AMOC is part of a global system of ocean circulation called the thermohaline circulation.

base load In electricity markets, base load refers to the continuous, steady demand that is always present, regardless of time of day or season. Power plants that provide base load supply have historically relied on coal, nuclear, and hydro generation that run continuously with low operating cost. With the introduction of even cheaper renewable sources to the grid, wind and solar are increasingly being combined with storage to provide base load.

biomass Organic material that comes from plants and animals; it is a renewable source of energy. Biomass may be used to generate power through combustion or in bioreactors that convert organic material into biofuels like ethanol, methane, and biodiesel. Bioreactors can also provide the feedstock for a variety of industrial and chemical processes.

bituminous coal The most commonly used type of coal globally, it is softer and dirtier than anthracite, but cleaner and more energy-dense than lignite. It is commonly used for electricity generation and steel making.

GLOSSARY 131

capacity factor In energy generation, the ratio of actual output from a power plant to its maximum capacity over a period of time. Because wind and solar energy are intermittent, they tend to have lower capacity factors than coal or nuclear.

cap-and-trade Cap-and-trade regimes set a cap on emissions for defined commitment periods, and issue only enough permits to cover those emissions. At the end of defined commitment periods, emitters must redeem permits corresponding to their emissions. Because permits may be traded, cap-and-trade systems encourage emissions reductions by firms with the lowest cost of reduction.

Carbon Border Adjustment Mechanism (CBAM) The European Union policy to prevent carbon leakage by imposing a carbon price on imported goods. The tax initially applies to energy-intensive imports including steel and fertilizer.

carbon budget The maximum amount of carbon dioxide emissions that can be emitted while keeping below a certain temperature threshold.

carbon capture and storage (CCS) A group of emerging technologies to capture and store carbon dioxide, typically from industrial processes. So-called clean coal power plants rely on carbon capture and storage to reduce their carbon emissions.

carbon cycle The natural process through which carbon is exchanged between the atmosphere, oceans, soil, and living organisms. At the heart of the carbon cycle is the interaction between plants and animals. Plants use photosynthesis to convert carbon dioxide into carbohydrates and other molecules that are the building blocks of life; animals consume plant molecules and release the carbon again as carbon dioxide.

carbon dioxide (CO_2)   A greenhouse gas that is a major contributor to global warming and climate change.

carbon dioxide equivalent (CO_2e)   A standardized measure of climate impact that allows scientists to compare different greenhouse gases based on their global warming potential.

Carbon Disclosure Project (CDP)   A popular nonprofit reporting platform that allows companies and cities to disclose their climate impact.

carbon insets   Carbon emissions reductions that occur within a company's supply chain. For companies that set Scope 3 emissions reduction targets, supplier emission reduction can be claimed as carbon insets.

carbon offsets   Certificates generated by reducing emissions of carbon dioxide or other greenhouse gases. Carbon offsets may be purchased or traded in order to compensate for emissions made elsewhere.

carbon premium   The additional amount that buyers are willing to pay for carbon-neutral or low-carbon products. (*See* willingness to pay.)

carbon pricing   A method to reduce global warming emissions by putting a price on carbon emissions that reflect its climate impact.

carbon sequestration   The process of capturing and storing atmospheric carbon dioxide.

GLOSSARY   **133**

certified emissions reduction (CER) A type of carbon credit issued under the Clean Development Mechanism of the Kyoto Protocol.

chlorofluorocarbons (CFCs) Chemical compounds that contribute to ozone depletion and are regulated under the Montreal Protocol.

Clean Air Act (1970) A US federal law designed to control air pollution on a national level.

Clean Development Mechanism (CDM) A mechanism under the Kyoto Protocol that allows industrialized countries to earn carbon credits for investments in emissions reduction projects in developing countries.

climate response scenario (CRS) A tool used by companies and governments to project the potential impacts of climate change and the effectiveness of mitigation strategies.

combined cycle gas turbine (CCGT) A highly efficient type of power plant that combines a gas turbine with a steam turbine to generate electricity.

compliance-grade offsets Carbon offsets that meet specific regulatory standards.

compliance period The time frame in which regulated entities must comply with emission reduction targets.

Conference of Parties (COP) The decision-making body of the United Nations Framework Convention on Climate Change, which meets annually to review progress in dealing with climate change.

134   GLOSSARY

convection cell   Areas in a fluid where warm liquid or gas rises and cool liquid or gas sinks. In the atmosphere, for example, heating at the equator causes air to rise, driving the tropical Hadley cell.

Coriolis effect   The deflection of moving objects when they are viewed in a rotating reference frame, such as on the surface of the Earth. The Coriolis effect causes north- and south-blowing winds in the Northern Hemisphere to deflect to the right. This effect drives both the trade winds and the prevailing westerlies.

Corporate Average Fuel Economy (CAFE)   Regulations in the United States aimed at improving the average fuel economy of cars and light trucks.

Corporate Sustainability Reporting Directive (CSRD)   A European Union directive that requires companies to disclose information on their environmental and social impacts.

direct air capture   A range of technologies to capture carbon dioxide directly from the atmosphere.

discount rate   The interest rate used to discount future cash flows to their present value.

Dynamic Integrated Climate-Economy (DICE) Model   A popular integrated assessment model (IAM) that combines economic and climate science projections to assess the impacts of climate change and policy responses.

emission reduction units (ERUs)   Units of greenhouse gas emission reduction generated by Joint Implementation projects under the Kyoto Protocol.

GLOSSARY

emissions-aligned compensation Firm pay strategies that include decarbonization as part of an employee's variable compensation in order to help meet emission-reduction targets.

energy balance model (EBM) A representation of the balance between incoming solar radiation and outgoing terrestrial radiation.

enteric emissions Methane emissions produced by the digestive processes of livestock. Ruminant livestock emissions represent nearly a third of all anthropogenic methane emissions.

environment, social, and governance (ESG) Criteria used to evaluate a company's operations and performance on environmental, social, and governance issues.

European Climate Law Adopted in 2021, a law that sets the framework for the European Union to achieve climate neutrality by 2050.

European taxonomy A classification system for environmentally sustainable economic activities in the European Union that provides the basis for climate-friendly finance, including the issuance of green bonds.

European Union Emissions Trading System (EU ETS) A cap-and-trade system launched in 2005 intended to reduce greenhouse gas emissions in the European Union.

externalities Costs or benefits that affect third parties that did not choose to incur those costs or benefits. The societal costs of climate change are an example of a negative externality caused by the emission of greenhouse gases.

GLOSSARY

feed-in tariff (FIT) A policy designed to accelerate investment in renewable energy deployment, especially solar and wind power, by providing producers with a guaranteed, above-market price over a long period, typically fifteen to twenty years.

Ferrel cell A mid-latitude atmospheric convection cell that lies between the Hadley cell and the polar cell. The Ferrel Cell causes winds to flow north and eastward between roughly 30° and 60° north latitude.

foraminifera (foram) Single-cell marine organisms found in sediment cores whose shells are used to measure historical ocean surface temperature.

forcing An external factor that influences the climate system, such as changes in solar radiation (natural forcing) or greenhouse gas concentration (human forcing).

general circulation model (GCM) A type of climate model that uses computational fluid dynamics equations to simulate flows of the Earth's atmosphere and oceans.

Global Reporting Initiative (GRI) An international organization that provides standards for sustainability reporting for corporations and governments.

global warming potential (GWP) A measure of how much heat a greenhouse gas traps in the atmosphere over a specific time period.

Green Deal A set of policy initiatives by the European Union aimed at making Europe climate-neutral by 2050.

GLOSSARY **137**

greenhouse effect The warming of the Earth's surface and atmosphere caused by the presence of greenhouse gases in the atmosphere.

greenhouse gas (GHG) Gases that trap heat in the atmosphere, contributing to the greenhouse effect. These include water vapor, carbon dioxide, methane, nitrous oxide, and other specialized gases such as hydrofluorocarbons (HFCs).

Hadley cell In models of the Earth's atmospheric circulation, a convection cell that features rising air near the equator and sinking air in the subtropics.

Henry Hub price The pricing point for natural gas futures contracts traded on the New York Mercantile Exchange. The Henry Hub is a gas pipeline distribution hub in Erath, Louisiana.

hydrocarbons Organic compounds consisting of hydrogen and carbon, found in fossil fuels.

ice core A core sample from the accumulation of snow and ice over many years that contains trapped air bubbles from past atmospheres. Ice cores from Greenland and Antarctica are used to detect temperature and atmospheric properties over the past 800,000 years.

Inflation Reduction Act A 2022 US federal law that included subsidies for renewable energy research, production, and demand.

integrated assessment model (IAM) A computer model that combines simulations of economic and geophysical systems to assess the interactions between humans and the climate. IAMs are used to assess climate policy tools and calculate optimal carbon tax levels.

Intergovernmental Panel on Climate Change (IPCC) An international body formed in 1988 to assess the science related to climate change. Assessment reports presenting its findings are published every six to seven years.

International Integrated Reporting Council (IIRC) A global coalition formed in 2010 to promote the Integrated Reporting Framework for corporate disclosure, which includes climate disclosures.

International Sustainability Standards Board (ISSB) An organization established in 2021 that develops global standards for sustainability reporting.

joint implementation (JI) A mechanism under the Kyoto Protocol that allows industrialized (Annex I) countries to earn carbon credits for investments in emission reduction projects in other industrialized countries.

just transition A framework for a fair and equitable shift to a low-carbon economy, ensuring that workers and communities are not left behind.

Kyoto Protocol An international treaty negotiated within the UN Framework Convention on Climate Change that commits its parties to reduce greenhouse gas emissions. Emissions reductions were defined for two commitment periods: 2008–2012, and 2013–2020.

leakage The phenomenon in which restrictions on greenhouse gas emissions in one country or region lead emitting companies to shift production to locations with lower standards.

GLOSSARY 139

levelized cost of electricity (LCOE) A measure of the average cost of electricity for a generating plant over its lifetime. The calculation combines the capital cost of constructing the facility with the operating costs associated with running it.

lignite A brownish-black coal with high moisture content, low energy density, and high ash production. Often called "brown coal," lignite is mostly used for electricity generation, and it emits more carbon dioxide than other coals.

load shedding The deliberate shutdown of electric power in parts of a grid when demand exceeds generation capacity, leading to blackouts.

loss and damages The impacts of climate change that cannot be avoided through mitigation or adaptation efforts.

marginal abatement cost curve (MACC) A graph that shows the cost of different measures to reduce greenhouse gas emissions by a company or country. Some abatement activities generate positive financial returns, while others generate negative returns.

methane (CH_4) A potent greenhouse gas with a global warming potential many times that of carbon dioxide. Methane is a stronger greenhouse gas than carbon dioxide, but it breaks down more rapidly in the atmosphere.

moral hazard The theory that individuals or organizations may take greater risks if they do not have to bear the full consequences of those risks. In the realm of climate change, it is often used to describe a concern that carbon removal or adaptation technologies could weaken efforts to reduce greenhouse gas emissions.

nationally determined contribution (NDC) Under the 2015 Paris Agreement, climate action plans submitted by countries outlining their efforts to reduce national emissions.

natural gas A fossil fuel, primarily methane, used as a source of energy for heating, cooking, and electricity generation.

net-zero target A goal set by countries and companies that defines the year when carbon emissions will be fully offset by carbon removal and/or carbon credits.

nitrous oxide (N_2O) A greenhouse gas with a high global warming potential, mostly produced by agriculture through the application of nitrogen-based synthetic fertilizers.

offset A reduction in emissions of carbon dioxide or other greenhouse gases made in order to compensate for emissions made elsewhere. Carbon offsets may be purchased or traded.

offtake agreement A contract between a producer and a buyer to purchase or sell portions of the producer's future production at a contracted price. Offtake agreements may be used by suppliers as collateral to finance green investments.

ozone (O_3) A molecule composed of three oxygen atoms, found in the Earth's stratosphere, which absorbs much of the sun's ultraviolet radiation.

Paris Agreement An international treaty adopted in 2015 to address climate change and its negative impacts, with the goal of limiting global warming to below 2°C above pre-industrial levels.

Unlike the binding emissions reductions required by the Kyoto Protocol, reductions under the Paris Agreement were set voluntarily through nationally determined contributions.

peak load   The period of maximum electrical power demand over the course of a day. Electrical grids commonly rely on gas power stations built specifically to service peak load periods, called "peakers." Storage such as pumped hydro and grid-scale batteries may also provide power during peak load.

permanence   A critical factor for carbon offsets, permanence describes the ability of a project to maintain its carbon sequestration benefits over time.

photovoltaic (PV)   Technology that converts sunlight directly into electricity using solar cells.

Pigouvian tax   A tax imposed on activities that generate negative externalities, intended to correct an inefficient market outcome. Named for the British welfare economist Arthur Pigou. Carbon taxes are an example of a Pigouvian tax.

power purchase agreement (PPA)   A long-term contract between two parties, one which generates electricity (the seller) and one which is purchasing the electricity (the buyer).

prevailing westerlies   Winds that blow from the West to the East in the midlatitudes.

public good   A commodity or service that is provided without charge to all members of a society, either by the government or by a private individual or organization. Formally, public goods are nonexclusive and nonrival, meaning anyone can use them, and use by one person does not reduce use by another. Lighthouses are a classic example, as is a healthy climate. Historically, public goods have tended to be underprovided.

pumped storage hydropower   A type of hydroelectric power generation used for load balancing, storing energy in the form of water pumped to a higher elevation.

radiant flux   The measure of the total power of electromagnetic radiation (including visible light) emitted from a source.

radiative forcing   The change in energy flux in the atmosphere due to changes in factors such as greenhouse gas concentrations.

Regional Greenhouse Gas Initiative (RGGI)   A cooperative effort among northeastern US states to reduce CO_2 emissions from the power sector. The goal is achieved through a cap-and-trade scheme.

representative concentration pathway (RCP)   A scenario that describes the emissions and concentrations of greenhouse gases. RCPs are used by policy makers to link projected greenhouse gas emissions to future temperature rise and climate impact. The IPCC's *2021 Sixth Assessment Report* described seven RCPs, ranging from the low-impact RCP1.9 to the high-impact RCP8.5.

resonant frequency   The frequency at which a system oscillates with maximum amplitude. Atmospheric gases that resonate at frequencies within the infrared gap absorb Earth's energy and cause the greenhouse effect.

GLOSSARY

science-based target A greenhouse gas reduction target that is aligned with the level of decarbonization required to keep global temperature increase below 1.5°C compared to preindustrial temperatures.

Science Based Targets initiative (SBTi) An organization that helps companies set science-based targets to reduce greenhouse gas emissions.

Scopes 1, 2, and 3 Categories of greenhouse gas emissions defined by the Greenhouse Gas Protocol: Scope 1 (direct emissions from owned or controlled sources), Scope 2 (indirect emissions from the generation of purchased electricity, steam, heating, and cooling), and Scope 3 (all other indirect emissions that occur in a company's value chain, including upstream suppliers and downstream users).

sequestration Any of a range of technologies for capturing and storing atmospheric carbon dioxide.

shared socioeconomic pathways (SSPs) Scenarios of projected socioeconomic global changes up to 2100, used to derive greenhouse gas emissions scenarios in light of different future climate policies.

social cost of carbon A measure of the economic harm from emitting one additional ton of carbon dioxide into the atmosphere. The social cost of carbon takes into account future climate damage, using a discount rate to convert it into current prices. Estimates of the social cost of carbon are used to determine optimal carbon tax rates.

Sustainability Accounting Standards Board (SASB) An organization founded in 2011 to develop and disseminate sustainability accounting disclosure standards.

Task Force on Climate-Related Financial Disclosures (TCFD) An organization that develops voluntary climate-related financial risk disclosures for use by companies in providing information to investors, lenders, and insurance underwriters.

thermal expansion The increase in volume of a substance due to an increase in temperature. Thermal expansion from warming oceans contributes to sea-level rise.

thermohaline circulation A large-scale ocean circulation that is driven by global density gradients created by surface heat (thermo) and salinity (haline).

Thwaites Glacier A large, rapidly changing glacier in West Antarctica that is contributing to sea-level rise, sometimes referred to as the "doomsday glacier."

tipping point A critical threshold at which a small change can lead to a drastic and irreversible effect on the environment. Examples of climate tipping points include thawing permafrost and deforestation of the Amazon rainforest.

trade winds Winds that consistently blow from east to west just north and south of the equator.

transpiration The process by which moisture is carried through plants from roots to small pores located mostly on the underside of leaves, where it changes to vapor and is released to the atmosphere. In tropical jungles, transpiration is an important source of atmospheric moisture.

UN Environment Programme (UNEP) An agency of the United Nations that coordinates its environmental activities and assists developing countries in implementing environmentally sound policies and practices.

UN Framework Convention on Climate Change (UNFCCC) An international treaty signed in 1992–1993 governing the United Nations negotiations to combat climate change by reducing greenhouse gas concentrations in the atmosphere.

UN Global Compact (UNGC) A nonbinding United Nations pact to encourage businesses worldwide to adopt sustainable and socially responsible policies.

UN Sustainable Development Goals (UN SDGs) A set of seventeen global goals established by the United Nations to address global challenges and achieve a better and more sustainable future for all. SDG 13 addresses climate change.

Verra A nonprofit organization that develops and manages standards for climate action and sustainable development. Verra certifies carbon offsets that qualify to meet the California Air Resources Board emissions limits.

West Texas Intermediate Light Sweet Crude Oil (WTI) A grade of crude oil that is used as a benchmark in oil pricing. The lower density (light) and lower sulfur content (sweet) of WTI tends to make it more expensive than other petroleum.

willingness to pay The additional amount an individual or household is willing to pay to support reducing greenhouse gas emissions. (*See* carbon premium).

NOTES

Chapter 2

1. PwC, *PwC's Voice of the Consumer Survey 2024: Shrinking the Consumer Trust Deficit*, May 15, 2024, https://www.pwc.com/gx/en/issues/c-suite-insights/voice-of-the-consumer-survey.html.

2. BCG, "Green Awakening: Are Consumers Open to Paying More for Decarbonized Products?," December 4, 2023, https://www.bcg.com/publications/2023/consumers-are-willing-to-pay-for-net-zero-production.

3. Unite Group, Applicant Survey, June 2021, https://www.unitegroup.com/wp-content/uploads/2021/10/Applicant-survey-June-2021-published-version-images.pdf.

4. KPMG, "Climate Quitting: Younger Workers Voting with their Feet on Employer's ESG Commitments," January 24, 2023, https://kpmg.com/uk/en/home/media/press-releases/2023/01/climate-quitting-younger-workers-voting-esg.html.

5. Emanuele Colonnelli et al., "Polarizing Corporations: Does Talent Flow to 'Good' Firms?," NBER working paper 31913, November 2023, https://doi.org/10.3386/w31913.

6. Ray A. Goldberg and Charlotte Tasker, "Nestlé: The World's Largest Food Company Confronts Climate Change," Case 922-302 (Boston: Harvard Business Publishing, 2021).

7. The founding organizations were the Climate Disclosure Project (CDP), World Resources Institute (WRI), the World Wide Fund for Nature (WWF), and the UN Global Compact (UNGC).

Chapter 3

1. The Kelvin (K) temperature scale sets 0° at absolute zero, the lowest possible temperature. It uses the same units as centigrade, so that 0°C equals 276°K. 6,000°K is *very* hot.

2. Chen Zhou et al., "Greater Committed Warming after Accounting for the Pattern Effect," *Nature Climate Change* 11 (2021): 132–136.

3. Aguo Dai and Kevin Trenberth, "Estimates of Freshwater Discharge from Continents: Latitudinal and Seasonal Variations," *Journal of Hydrometeorology* 3 (2002), 660.

4. Isaac Newton, *Philosophiae Naturalis Principia Mathematica* (London: Jussu Societatis Regia ac Typus J. Streator, 1687), 12–13.

5. Scientists also use a range of other sources, including the history and composition of tree rings (dendrochronology), historical samples of pollen (palynology), past coral reefs, and mineral deposits (speleothems) that accumulate gradually over time in caves.

6. Because GCMs are so computationally intensive, IAMs typical rely on simplified climate models that summarize the outputs of the GCMs.

Chapter 4

1. Dirk Schoenmaker and Willem Schramade, "Which Discount Rate for Sustainability?," *Journal of Sustainable Finance and Accounting* 3, September 2024, https://doi.org/10.1016/j.josfa.2024.100010.

2. William Nordhaus, "Evolution of Modeling of the Economics of Global Warming: Changes in the DICE Model, 1992–2017," *Climatic Change* 148, no. 4 (2018): 623–640.

3. Schoenmaker and Schramade, "Which Discount Rate for Sustainability?"

4. Some countries that employ carbon taxes—like Mexico and South Africa—are experimenting with allowing carbon offsets to be used for payment of their tax bill, but this is still relatively uncommon.

5. Joeri Rogelj et al., "Net-Zero Emissions Targets Are Vague: Three Ways to Fix," *Nature*, March 16, 2021.

Chapter 5

1. Evan Mills, "Global Kerosene Subsidies: An Obstacle to Energy Efficiency and Development," *World Development* 99, no. 12 (2017): 463–480.

2. John Weaver, "More Solar Panels per Acre," *PV Magazine*, January 20, 2022.

3. Vladimir Vidović, et al., "Review of the Potentials for Implementation of Floating Solar Panels on Lakes and Water Reservoirs," *Renewable and Sustainable Energy Reviews* 178 (2023): 113237.

Chapter 6

1. Global Energy Monitor, "China's Coal Power Spree Could See over 300 Coal Plants Added before Emissions Peak," press release, August 28, 2023, https://globalenergymonitor.org/press-release/chinas-coal-power-spree-could-see-over-300-coal-plants-added-before-emissions-peak/.

INDEX

abatement, 16–17, 28–29
ACCESS template, 10–18
accounting, 15–16, 21, 23–29, 111–112
accounting firms, 1, 24
adaptation, to climate change, 10, 31, 36, 53, 61–62, 113, 125
Adaptation Fund, 108
additionality, 77, 78–79
adiabatic cooling, 57
advocacy, 22
Africa, 86
agriculture, 56, 57, 58, 62, 66
air, moisture in, 55–56
air capture technologies, 80
air conditioning, 95
air currents, 45–49
airlines, 96, 99
air pollution, 67–68
Alaska pipeline, 86
albedo, 38–39
anaerobic bacteria, 66
angular momentum, 48
animals, 64
Annex I countries, 108, 109
Antarctica, 50, 51, 59–60
anthracite, 90
Arctic, 42, 43, 44, 65
Arctic cell, 46–47
Arctic Ocean, 44, 45
Argo program, 44
aridity, 55–58, 92
asphalt, 65, 88
assessment, of physical risk, 11–12

assigned amount units (AAUs), 108
Atacama Desert, 57
Atlantic Meridional Overturning Circulation (AMOC), 44–45, 61
atmospheric air flows, 43–49
auto industry, 30
aviation fuel, 16, 99

Bangladesh, 7
base load, 94–96
batteries, 5, 16, 29, 96
    EV, 4, 85, 100, 122
    lithium-ion, 100
battery storage, 7, 96
Biden administration, 73, 115
bilateral agreements, 110, 127, 128
biofuels, 12
biomass, 94, 118
bioreactors, 29, 94
bituminous coal, 90
blackouts, 94
blue-green algae, 65, 89
BMW, 16
boards of directors, 1, 5, 22, 32
boreal forests, 65
Brazil, 4, 123, 128
British thermal unit (Btu), 89
brown coal, 90
brownouts, 94
butane, 65

150   INDEX

CAFE standards, 71, 115
California
  Air Resource Board, 116
  aridity in, 57
  cap-and-trade program in, 73, 77, 78, 116
  Central Valley and Inland Empire, 57
Canada, 107, 109, 116
capacity factor, 97
cap-and-trade programs, 73–78, 106, 108–110, 116–118, 128
capital costs
  of fossil fuels, 99–100
  of renewable energy, 96–99
carbon, 63
  social cost of, 67–73
  stores of, 65
carbon accounting, 15–16, 21, 23–29, 111–112
Carbon Border Adjustment Mechanism (CBAM), 13, 30, 119
carbon budget, 63–64, 73–76
carbon capture and storage (CCS), 80, 99, 119
carbon cycle, 64–67
carbon dioxide (CO_2), 40, 41, 63, 64
  absorption, 39
  from fossil fuels, 90
  historical data on, 50–51
  regulation of, 115–116
  release of, 65–66
  warming effect of, 66–67
Carbon Disclosure Project (CDP), 24, 25
carbon emissions. *See* greenhouse gas emissions
Carboniferous Age, 64, 90
carbon insets, 13, 81
carbon market, 63–81, 116–118
  See also cap-and-trade programs
carbon neutrality, 118–119
carbon offsets, 27, 76–81, 109, 117

carbon pricing, 63, 81
  debate over, 71, 72
  discount rate and, 69–73
carbon sequestration, 16–17, 76–77, 79, 80, 119
carbon storage. *See* carbon capture and storage
carbon taxes, 5–6, 13, 68, 70–74, 81, 119
carbon trading. *See* cap-and-trade programs
cellulose, 64
certified emissions reductions (CERs), 78–79, 109–110
chemicals industry, 13, 18, 32
chief executive officers (CEOs), 1, 2, 20
  leadership by, 22–24
  regulators and, 31
Chile, 4, 57
China, 46, 56
  cap-and-trade programs in, 73–74
  electric vehicles in, 121–122
  green industrial policy in, 120–122, 123
  Kyoto Protocol and, 108, 109, 110
  Paris Agreement and, 111
  renewable energy innovation in, 5, 79
CHIPS and Science Act, 116
chlorofluorocarbons (CFCs), 105–106
circulation flows, 43–49
Clean Air Act, 115
Clean Development Mechanism (CDM), 79, 109
clean energy companies, 4
Clean Power Plan (CPP), 116
climate, as public good, 103–104
climate change
  adaptation to, 10, 31, 36, 53, 61–62, 113, 125
  corporate response to, 9–33
  fossil fuels and, 90–92
  human response to, 37–38, 52–55, 61–62

INDEX

impacts and costs of, 11–12, 54–55, 67–73, 104

misinformation about, 36–37

policy responses to, 1–4, 103–123

regional approaches to, 113–122

science of, 2, 3, 35–62

climate cycles, historical, 50–52

climate data, historical, 49–52

climate denialism, 20, 55

Climate Disclosure Standards Board (CDSB), 25

climate entrepreneurs, 8, 128

climate-friendly products, willingness to pay for, 12–15, 21

climate investments, 4, 21, 30

climate justice, 80, 106, 108, 113, 128

climate leadership, 5–7, 22–24

climate modeling, 37–55, 61

energy balance model, 37, 38–42, 61

general circulation model, 37, 42–52, 61

integrated assessment models, 38, 52–55, 61, 69

climate response scenario (CRS) planning, 17–18

climate science, 35–62, 55–59

climate modeling, 37–55

reasons for understanding, 35–37

weather, 55–59

climate skeptics, 20, 55

Clinton administration, 115

cloud cover, 39

cloud formation, 49, 61

Clouds and Earth Radiant Energy System (CERES), 41

CO_2 scrubbers, 80

coal, 7, 65, 68, 89–92, 95, 97, 116, 120

coal mines, 7, 89, 90

coal plants, 84, 96, 98, 116, 118

coal producers, 75

combined cycle gas turbines (CCGT), 94

commercial airlines, 96

Commission on Sustainable Development, 106

compensation, linking to green outcomes, 19

competition, 10, 14–15

competitors, cooperation among, 21

compliance-grade offsets, 77–78

computer simulations, 49–50

Conference of Parties (COP), 106–107, 110

construction industry, 62

convection, 45–47, 49

Convention on Biological Diversity, 106

coordination, lack of, 103–104

Coriolis effect, 47–49, 60

corporate accounting, 69–70

Corporate Average Fuel Emissions (CAFE) standards, 71, 115

corporate culture, 19, 20

corporate strategy, 126–127

Corporate Sustainability Reporting Directive (CSRD), 25, 26, 119

cost-benefit analyses, for regulations, 71, 73

Covid–19 pandemic, 72

criticism, of carbon offsets, 78–81

crude oil, 65, 85–88

cultural transformation, 19, 20

customers, 1, 12–13, 21, 24

dams, 58, 92

data, climate, 49–52

decarbonization, 3, 6

benefits of, 8

challenges for firms, 126–128

decision-making on, 5, 125–126

drivers of, 12

of electrical grids, 99–100

investments in, 4, 21, 30

leadership of, 5–7, 22–24

opposition to, 20

risks of, 17–18

of supply chains, 15–17

deforestation, 64, 65

deluges, 55, 56

desalination plants, 99
desertification, 56
developing countries
  carbon border taxes and, 119
  climate change mitigation in, 17
  climate justice and, 104–105
  economic development in, 7
  Kyoto Protocol and, 108, 109, 120
  Paris Agreement and, 113
  petroleum industry in, 88
  renewable energy and, 99, 100, 123
diesel, 88, 91
direct carbon capture, 99
disclosure standards, 24–27
discount rate, 69–73
double counting, of carbon offsets, 79
Dynamic Integrated Climate-
  Economy (DICE) model, 54–55

Earth
  equator, 37, 42–45, 46
  poles, 42–46
  rotation of, 48
Earth Summit, 106
easterly trade winds, 49
electrical utilities, load balancing by,
  94–96
electricity
  price of, 85, 96–97, 118
  supply and demand for, 94–96
  transmission of, 100
electricity generation
  cost of, 85, 123
  emissions from, 83–84
  from fossil fuels, 85–90
  load balancing, 94–96
  measurement of, 84–85
  from renewable sources, 92–94,
  96–98, 118
electricity storage, 100
Electric Reliability Council of Texas
  (ERCOT), 94
electric vehicles (EVs), 4, 5, 121–122
electromagnetic radiation, 38–40

emission reduction units (ERUs),
  108–109
emissions. *See* greenhouse gas
  emissions
emissions permits, 73–76, 108,
  110–111, 117
emissions reduction targets, 13–14,
  27–28, 105–112, 116–119
emissions standards
  aligning compensation with, 19
  European, 5–6
  higher, 30
emissions trading. *See* cap-and-trade
  programs
Emissions Trading System. *See*
  European Union Emissions
  Trading System (EU ETS)
employees, 1, 15
energy
  from fossil fuels, 85–92
  generation, economics of, 98–99
  renewable, 3, 7, 75, 79, 83–101, 109,
  120–123
energy balance model (EBM), 37,
  38–42, 61
energy consumption
  increase in, 83–84
  measurement of, 84–85
energy-efficient products, 12–14
energy prices, 94, 96–97
energy system, load balancing,
  94–96
enteric emissions, 66
environmental, social, and governance (ESG) groups, 22
environmental protection
  in Germany, 118
  in United States, 114–116
Environmental Protection Act, 115
Environmental Protection Agency,
  115–116
environmental regulations, 71, 73
environmental reporting standards,
  24–27
equator, 42–46

INDEX

ERCOT. *See* Electric Reliability
Council of Texas (ERCOT)
ethane, 65, 87–88
ethanol, 128
Europe
approaches to climate change in,
113, 114
corporate responses in, 14, 17, 30, 31
decarbonization in, 5–6, 12, 13
decline in emissions in, 118
impact of climate change in, 56–57
palm oil industry and, 14
renewable energy in, 128
European Climate Law, 119
European Union
carbon offsets in, 78–79
disclosure standards in, 25, 26
emissions permits in, 75
emissions reduction targets in, 107
emissions trading in, 73, 74,
109–110, 117–118
response to climate change in,
117–120
European Union Emissions Trading
System (EU ETS), 13, 73, 74, 76,
109–110, 117–118
EV batteries, 4, 85, 100, 122
experimentation, 19
externalities, 68, 72
external organization, 20–22
extraction costs, oil, 86–87
extraction technologies, 87
extreme heat, 55

factory smoke, 67, 68
feedback effects, 51–52
feed-in tariffs, 98, 118
Ferrel cell, 46–47, 49, 56
fertilizer, 99
financial subsidies, 7, 30, 103, 116,
121, 122, 123
firms
collaboration among, 21
incumbent, 18–19, 31–32

NGOs and, 21–22
relationships with regulators, 29–32
"Fit for 55," 118–119
flaring, 87–88
flexibility mechanisms, 108, 109, 113
flooding, 56, 59
food waste, 66
foraminifera (forams), 50
forcing, 38, 53
forest clearing, 14
forest fires, 56–57, 79
forests, 79–80
Forest Stewardship Council, 22
fossil fuels, 3, 7
advantages of, 92
burning of, 42, 51, 52, 65, 69, 83,
90–91
capital costs of, 99–100
climate change and, 90–92
coal, 7, 65, 68, 89–92, 95, 97, 116, 120
country differences in, 113–114
electricity generation from, 85–90
emissions from, 90–92
natural gas, 65, 66, 87–91, 116
petroleum, 65, 85–88
transition to green energy from,
3–5, 11–12, 83–101
fracking, 87
fractionating column, 87
Framework Convention on Climate
Change (FCCC). *See* UN
Framework Convention on
Climate Change (UNFCCC)
France, 114, 117
free riding, 104
fuel efficiency standards, 71, 73, 115
fusion generation, 5, 99
future cost estimates, 69
futures markets
for natural gas, 89
for oil, 87

gas. *See* natural gas
gasoline, 86, 88

154 INDEX

gasoline subsidies, 7
gas pipelines, 89
gas turbines, 94
General Agreement on Tariffs and
    Trade (GATT), 127
general circulation model (GCM), 37,
    42–52, 61
geopolitical conflicts, 96
geothermal energy, 5, 93, 98
Germany, 114, 117, 118
gigawatts (GW), 84
glaciers, 58–60
global carbon budget, 63–64, 74–75
global competition, 127–128
Global Reporting Initiative (GRI),
    24–26
global sea levels, 11, 51–52, 55, 59–60
Global South, 104–105
global supply chains, 6
global temperature rise
    projection on future, 71, 72
    rising tides and, 59–60
    source of, 41
    targets for, 75, 107, 111, 118
    weather patterns and, 55–59
global warming potential (GWP),
    66–67
Gobi Desert, 4
"Golden Sun" initiative, 121
government agencies, interactions
    with, 29–32
government responses. *See* policy
    responses
green ammonia, 99
Green Deal, 119
green economy, 7
green energy transition, 3, 11–12,
    83–101
    Kyoto Protocol and, 108–109
    navigating, 4–5
    opportunities from, 8
    uncertainty around, 125–126
green fuels, 96, 99, 128
greenhouse effect, 40, 66, 90
Greenhouse Gas (GHG) Protocol, 27

greenhouse gas emissions
    from China, 120
    decline in Europe, 118
    decline in US, 116
    economics of, 3
    from fossil fuels, 90–92
    reduction of, 1, 2, 13
    regulation of, 73–74
    sources of, 64–67, 83
    standards for, 5
    targets for reducing, 13–14, 27–28,
        105–112, 116–119
    trading, 73–78, 106, 108–110,
        116–118
greenhouse gases, 64–67
Greenland, 50, 59–60
Green Party, 114, 117, 118
green premium, 12–15, 21
green technologies. *See*
    technologies
greenwashing, 22, 26–27
grid-scale battery storage, 96,
    100
Gulf of Mexico, 86

Hadley, George, 46
Hadley cell, 46–47, 49
halogenated hydrocarbons (halons),
    66, 105–106
heat capacity, 42
heating buildings, 83
"heavy" crude, 86
Henry Hub, 89
HFC-23, 109–110
historical climate data, 49–52
horizontal drilling, 87
Hornsea 2 wind farm, 84
hurricanes, 55, 60
hydraulic fracturing, 87
hydrocarbons, 63, 65, 66, 85–88,
    90–91
hydroelectric power, 92
hydrofluorocarbons (HFCs), 67
hydrogen technologies, 30

INDEX

ice ages, 50–51
ice cores, 50
ice sheets, melting, 59–60
incumbent firms
    decarbonization by, 18–19, 32
    regulators and, 31
India, 6, 57, 74, 79, 108, 109, 122, 123
indigenous people, 7
Indonesia, 14
industrialization, 7
    environmental impact of, 67–68
    second wave of, 127, 128
industrialized countries, 104–105, 108, 113
industrial policy
    in China, 120–122
    global, 122–123
industrial revolution, 65, 127
industry
    energy needs of, 83
    relocating, near energy sources, 101
industry associations, 21, 31
Inflation Reduction Act, 30, 116
infrared gap, 40–41
infrared radiation, 40–43, 66
innovation, 20, 32, 98, 127
insurance, 62
    companies, 31
    costs, 11
    risk, 31
integrated assessment models (IAMs), 38, 52–55, 61, 69
integrated reporting (IR) framework, 25, 26
interest rates, 70, 99
intergenerational justice, 104
Intergovernmental Panel on Climate Change (IPCC), 3–4, 52–53, 76, 79, 103, 107
internal combustion engine, 113
International Business Council, 26

International Federation of Accountants, 26
International Financial Reporting Standards (IFRS), 25
International Integrated Reporting Council (IIRC), 26
international trade, 127–128
investors, 5, 24–27
irrigation, 58

Jakobshavn Glacier, 60
Japan, 30, 107, 109, 114, 128
job losses, 20
joint implementation (JI), 108–109
just transition, 105

kerosene, 86, 88, 96
kilowatt hours (KWh), 85
Kyoto Protocol, 4, 78, 103, 105–111, 115, 117, 120, 122

latitude, Earth energy balance by, 42–43
lawmakers, 31
leaders, 1–2, 20, 31, 128
leadership
    climate, 5–7, 22–24, 32, 128
    role for, 4–5
leakage, 75
learning, 19
legacy firms, decarbonization by, 18–19
levelized cost of electricity (LCOE), 96–98
"light" crude, 86
lignin, 64
lignite, 90
liquid fuels, 88
liquid natural gas (LNG), 89
lithium-ion batteries, 100
load balancing, 94–96, 98

156 INDEX

load shedding, 94
lobbying, 30, 31

managers
  as leaders of green transition, 128
  resistance from, 19
manufacturing firms, 32
marginal abatement cost curve (MACC), 28–29, 126
marginalized groups, 7
marine plankton, 50
Marrakesh Partnership for Global Climate Action (MPGCA), 112–113
matrix organizations, 19–20
megawatt hours (MWh), 85
megawatts (MW), 84
methane (CH_4), 40, 41, 63, 65, 66
  absorption, 39
  combustion of, 90–91
  extraction of, 87–88
  measuring emissions of, 69
  natural gas from, 88–89
  warming effect of, 67
Microsoft, 26
Middle East, 86
middle-income countries, 108–109
minerals, mining, and processing, 4
Mississippi River basin, 58
Montreal Protocol, 105–106, 108
moral hazard, 61–62
Morocco, 4
mountain snowpack, 57–58

NASA, 41
national climate champions, 112
nationally determined contributions (NDCs), 111–112
national responses, to climate change, 113–122
national targets, 33, 113, 116, 119, 121

natural gas, 65, 87–90, 116
  combustion of, 90–91
  distribution, 89
  from methane, 66, 87
  prices, 89, 97
natural gas plants, 98
natural resources, 4
Nestlé, 8, 16–17, 66
net-zero emissions, 13, 16, 21, 23, 28, 76, 78, 111
Net-Zero Insurance Alliance, 31
Nigeria, 88
nitrogen, 40
nitrous oxide (N_2O), 66, 67
nongovernmental organizations, 5, 21–22
nonstate actors, 112–113
Nordhaus, William, 54, 70–71
North Atlantic Ocean, 44, 49
Northern Hemisphere, 46, 56
North Sea, 86
north-south winds, 48–49
no-till farming, 79
nuclear power, 114, 117
nuclear reactors, 93, 97–99, 118

Obama administration, 73, 115–116
ocean currents, 43–45
oceans
  energy absorbed by, 42
  surface temperature, 50–51
offsets. *See* carbon offsets
offshore wind turbines, 93
offtake agreements, 16, 21
oil, 7, 12, 65, 66
  deposits, 86
  extraction costs, 86–87
  global production of, 118
  petroleum, 65, 85–88
  prices, 87
  refining, 86, 87
OPEC, 118
operating costs, of renewable energy, 96–98

INDEX

operational risk, 11–12
organization, 18–22
  external, 20–22
organizational siloes, 19–20
oxygen, 40, 64
ozone, 66
ozone layer, 105–106, 108

palm oil industry, 14
paraffins, 65, 88
Paris Agreement, 4, 28, 53, 64, 75, 81, 103, 105, 110–113, 115, 118, 119, 122
peak load, 94–96
peat bogs, 14
pension funds, 5
permafrost, 65, 72
permanence, 77, 80
petroleum, 65, 85–88
photosynthesis, 64
photovoltaics (PV), 5, 29, 92–93, 97, 121
physical risk assessment, 11–12
Pigou, Arthur, 68
Pigouvian tax, 68
plant-based fuels, 99
plant transpiration, 49
plastics, 88
polar ice, 39
policy responses, 3–6, 103–123
  in China, 120–122
  in Europe, 113, 114, 117–120
  Kyoto Protocol, 78, 103, 105–111, 115, 117, 120, 122
  Montreal Protocol, 105–106
  Paris Agreement, 28, 53, 64, 75, 81, 103, 105, 110–113, 115, 118, 119, 122
  regional approaches, 113–122
  role of United Nations in, 104
  UN framework, 105–113
  in United States, 114–116
political partisanship, 31–32, 114–115
political risk, 31–32
political systems, 114

pollution, 67–68
polyethylene (PE) plastics, 88
poor countries. *See* developing countries
portfolio risk, 26
Portugal, 117
power, 84–85
power plants, 84, 98, 116, 118
power purchase agreements (PPAs), 4, 95
prevailing westerlies, 49
profitability, 32
protectionism, 119
public goods, 103–104
public policies, 31–32
  See also policy responses
pumped hydropower, 95

radiant flux, 41
radiative forcing, 53
rainfall, 55–58
rainforests, 58–59, 65
refrigerant manufacturers, 109
regional climates, 49
Regional Greenhouse Gas Initiative (RGGI), 73, 74, 76, 116
regional weather conditions, 55–59
regulations, 13, 17, 29–32, 71, 73
regulators, 24, 29–32
relocation, of industries, 127
renewable energy, 3, 75, 79, 92–94
  See also specific types
  advantages of, 92, 96–99
  in China, 120–121
  costs and benefits of, 96–99
  in developing countries, 109
  investment in, 99–100, 120
  load balancing and, 95–96, 98
  potential of, 7
  storage technologies, 96
  subsidies for, 98, 116, 118, 121–123
  technologies, 5
  transition to, 3–5, 83–101
  transmission capacity of, 95

158 INDEX

renewable resources, 4
representative concentration
pathways (RCPs), 53–54
research, government funding
of, 30
reservoirs, 58
resistance, to organizational change,
19
resonant frequencies, 40
return on investment, 69–70
risk assessment, 11–12
risk management, 17–18
risk-taking, 19, 32
river pollution, 67
Russia, 89, 108, 109

Saudi Arabia, 86
Scandinavia, 4
scenarios, 17–18, 38
Science-Based Targets initiative
(SBTi), 28, 78
Scope 1 emissions, 15, 27, 119
Scope 2 emissions, 15, 27
Scope 3 emissions, 15, 27
sea-level rise, 11, 51–52, 55, 59–60
sequestration. *See* carbon
sequestration
shale gas, 116
shared socioeconomic pathways
(SSPs), 52–54
Siberia, 86
Sixth Assessment Report (IPCC), 53,
76, 107, 111
skilled workers, 4–5, 15
slave trade, 49
Smith, Adam, 67
snow volume, 58
social cost of carbon, 67–73
social justice, 7–8
solar energy, 41, 42, 92–93, 95, 121,
123
SOLAR framework, 3, 9–10
accounting, 24–29
leadership, 22–24

organization, 18–22
regulation, 29–32
strategy, 10–18
solar photovoltaic panels, 5, 29,
92–93, 97, 121
solar power, 4, 7, 98, 118
solar radiation, 37–39, 41–43,
49
Solvay, 14
"sour" crude, 86
South Africa, 7
South Atlantic Ocean, 44
Southern Hemisphere, 46
South Korea, 128
Soviet Union, 106
spectral intensity, 39
spot markets
for coal, 90
for natural gas, 89
for oil, 87
stakeholders, 1, 24, 26
Starbucks, 11
steel industry, 13, 18, 31
Stegra, 16
Stern, Nicholas, 70
storage technologies, 96,
100
storm intensification, 60
storm surges, 11, 59
strategic assessments, 32
strategy, 10–18
subsidies, 7, 30, 103, 116, 121, 122,
123
sulfur, 63, 86, 87
supercomputers, 44
suppliers, 13, 15–17, 21, 27
supply chains, 12, 15–17, 21, 30
surface temperature, 50–51
surge pricing, 94
Sustainability Accounting Standards
Board (SASB), 25
sustainability committees, 22
sustainability officers, 5
"sweet" crude, 86
"sweet light" crude, 86

INDEX

159

tar, 88
target setting, 27–28
tariffs, 122
Task Force on Climate-Related
 Financial Disclosures (TCFD), 25
taxes, carbon, 5–6, 13, 68, 70–74, 81,
 119
technologies
 battery, 96
 carbon capture, 80
 extraction, 87
 green, 120–122
 hydrogen, 30
 investments in, 4, 19
 renewable energy, 5, 123
 storage, 96, 100
temperature fluctuations, 50–51
temperature rise. *See* global temperature rise
Texas, 4, 86, 95
thermal expansion, 60
thermal inertia, 42
thermohaline circulation, 44–45
Thwaites Glacier, 51–52, 60
tides, rising, 59–60
tipping point, 51–52, 72
Title Transfer Facility (TTF), 89
tradeable permits, 73–76
trade agreements, 127
trade winds, 49
transmission grids, 95
transpiration, 58–59
transportation industry, 62, 83
trees, 65
tropical forests, 58–59, 65
Trump administration, 73, 115, 116
trust, building, 23–24
tundra, 65
two-party political systems, 114

Ukraine, 89
uncertainty, 23, 31, 125–126
UN Environmental Programme
 (UNEP), 26

UN Framework Convention on
 Climate Change (UNFCCC),
 106–107
UN Global Compact (UNGC), 26
United Kingdom, 72
United Nations, 104, 105–113
United States, 5
 bilateral climate accords by, 110
 decline in emissions in, 116
 electricity consumption in, 84, 85
 electricity rates in, 85
 emissions trading in, 73, 74
 fossil fuel reserves of, 114
 industrialization in, 127
 Kyoto Protocol and, 108, 109, 115
 natural gas prices in, 89
 political partisanship in, 31,
 114–115
 political system in, 114
 response to climate change in,
 114–116
 subsidies in, 30
UN Sustainable Development Goals
 (UN SDGs), 24–25, 26
US Army Corps of Engineers
 (USACE), 71
US Navy, 11–12

vegetation, 65
Verra, 77, 79

Walmart, 13
water, 90
 currents, 43–44
 heat capacity of, 42
 from methane combustion, 91
 thermal expansion of, 60
 vapor, 39, 40, 41
weather
 local, 49
 patterns, 44, 45, 55–59
westerly winds, 49
West Texas, 4, 86, 95

160   INDEX

West Texas Intermediate (WTI), 87
wildfires, 56–57
willingness to pay, 12–15, 21
wind power, 4, 7
winds, 43–49
wind turbines, 84, 92–93, 95, 97–98,
    116, 118, 121, 123
workers, skilled, 4–5, 15

World Business Council for Sustain-
    able Development, 27
World Economic Forum, 26
World Meteorological Organization,
    107
World Resources Institute, 27
World Trade Organization, 119
World Wildlife Fund, 5, 22

ACKNOWLEDGMENTS

This book began as a set of technical notes for my students who were taking the elective MBA course Global Climate Change. The book relies heavily on what I've learned from my colleagues in the Business, Government, and International Economy (BGIE) unit at Harvard Business School. I would especially like to thank my colleague Forest Reinhardt, who taught me more about the economics of climate change than anyone else and with whom I wrote an HBS case study on climate change. I also want to thank my colleague Dick Vietor, who with Forest has been a leader in studying and teaching about the business response to climate change at HBS. I am especially grateful to Dick and to Joe Lassiter, Cynthia Montgomery, and Andrew Winston for reading and commenting on the manuscript.

Jeff Kehoe, my editor at Harvard Business Review Press, was incredibly patient and supportive throughout the writing and editing process. His guidance helped me shape the book to address a broad managerial audience.

Much of the book synthesizes an established literature on the science, economics, and politics of climate change. Chapter 2 is different. This chapter describes the current state of the corporate response to climate change, drawing heavily on conversations I had with countless executives who are at the forefront of that effort. While I cannot name them all, I am incredibly grateful for their generosity in sharing their successes, their challenges, and their thoughtful approaches to this issue. They also helped set the tone of the book, which is more optimistic than much of the current literature on the topic.

Finally, I want to thank my wife, Seema Tikare, and my children, Freya and Taj, for their support and love during the weeks and months I worked on this book. Through this process I hope that our response to climate change today will ensure my children a brighter tomorrow.

ABOUT THE AUTHOR

GUNNAR TRUMBULL is the Philip Caldwell Professor of Business Administration at Harvard Business School. He earned his undergraduate degree in history and literature at Harvard College and his PhD in political science at MIT. Since then he has taught MBA and executive students in topics related to political economy and climate change at HBS. His research focuses on the politics of market regulation. Previous works include *Strength in Numbers* and *Consumer Capitalism*.